PENGUIN ANANDA

THE MUSK SYNDROME

A devotee of Sai Baba of Shirdi, Ruzbeh N. Bharucha is one of the most influential spiritual writers of our times. He is the author of fifteen books, including the bestselling Fakir trilogy, which has been translated into several languages. In 2014, *Rabda: My Sai . . . My Sigh,* published by Penguin Books, was an instant bestseller.

Formerly a journalist, he is also a documentary film-maker. His documentary *Sehat . . . Wings of Freedom,* on AIDS and HIV in Tihar Jail, was selected and screened at the XVII International AIDS Conference in 2008. His collaboration with Zambhala—India's yoga, music and life spirit festival, the first of its kind—gave birth to a series of powerful videos called 'Ramblings with Ruzbeh Bharucha'. His articles have been published in the *Times of India, Free Press Journal, Indian Express, Maharashtra Herald, Sunday Observer, Jam-e-Jamshed* and *Afternoon.* His book *My God Is a Juvenile Delinquent* has been included in the reading list of all judicial academies. Ruzbeh is the 110th Master for the 'Speaking Tree', where he writes an immensely popular blog on spirituality.

His Facebook page has reached out to thousands in a very short span of time. The daily affirmations and messages are a source of inspiration to many. He lives with his family in Pune.

You can reach him here:
Facebook: www.facebook.com/ruzbehbharucha
Twitter: @ruzbehnbharucha
Website: www.ruzbehbharucha.net
YouTube: www.youtube.com/channel/UCo-rFxiF7R9qaMMWdpj5fJQ

the musk syndrome

Ruzbeh N. Bharucha

Why Do You Look Elsewhere?
All That You Seek Is Within You

PENGUIN
ANANDA

An imprint of Penguin Random House

PENGUIN ANANDA

USA | Canada | UK | Ireland | Australia
New Zealand | India | South Africa | China

Penguin Ananda is part of the Penguin Random House group of companies
whose addresses can be found at global.penguinrandomhouse.com

Published by Penguin Random House India Pvt. Ltd
4th Floor, Capital Tower 1, MG Road,
Gurugram 122 002, Haryana, India

First published in Penguin Ananda by Penguin Random House India 2016

ISBN 9780143423850

Typeset in Adobe Garamond Pro by Manipal Digital Systems, Manipal

Printed at Repro India Limited

www.penguin.co.in

To

The Universal Mother Goddess and our Creator

Sai Baba of Shirdi

All Divine, Perfect, Ancient, Ascended Masters

Archangels and Angels

Celestial, Terrestrial, Physical Warriors of Light

The Oneness Family

Contents

Author's Note

I believe in the Creator. I believe the Creator is Pure Energy. According to me, the first manifestation of that energy is the form of Goddess Kali. For if there is a Creator, then that Creator holds the power of destruction or transformation or change. Thus for me, the Creator is formless but The One who is responsible for all change and all transformation has a form and that form is Mother Kali.

What pleases Kali the most? Pure love. When the individual destroys all false ego, stops all shadow dancing with himself/herself, annihilates everything but pure love for The One, that makes Kali smile and dance and embrace the seeker.

The only way to go about this is to begin the journey within. Still the mind, the heart and all thoughts, either by being completely in the moment, through chants, becoming one with the breath or in any manner that makes you still from within. The journey inward then commences, which eventually will lead to the warm embrace of The One.

Of course each one of us has his/her own interpretation of Creation and who the Creator is; I guess in our own way we shall be right and partially away from the real picture.

But whichever religion or ideology you and I profess to follow or believe, the fact remains that if we believe in a power beyond the beyond, then everything has come forth from that power. If everything has come forth from it, then that power resides in each and every one of us. If you and I are created by The One, then we imbibe within us The One. It maybe in a very dormant state or miniaturized state and not in that same dynamic magnitude, but each one of us has to have within us all that the Creator embodies or the same Divine Presence.

Somewhere in the by-lanes of our journey, some time in our many lifetimes, we have gravitated to the external, thus slowly shifting the Divine One further away from us. The Divine One is eternal but internal. In the form of the Spirit. The Spark from that Great Flame. And the more we go external, the dimmer this light shines within, till a time comes when the dust of the external buries this light within to a mere flicker.

Whatever I have learnt through channelling, prayers, reflection, hallucination, call it what you will, I have realized that heaven, hell, purgatory—all lie within each one of us.

We will gravitate towards what we choose and what we give priority to. Eventually, whatever our priority is in this lifetime or the next, some time in our journey, we shall be granted the realization of that priority. Thus the sages have told us time and again to be wary of what one truly desires, as just as sure as the morning dew, the thunder after the lightening, the decaying of the body or the purity of the fire, our wishes shall be granted no matter how profound or trivial, holy or debased, wise or absolutely insane.

One night, Agastya Rishi, that great sage, for some reason appeared in my dream and with a smile said, 'The Goddess Eternal, The One who is always in meditation, The One that Shiva Himself calls Bhagwati, The One who is forever in meditation, who is in the form of a peaceful Goddess Kali, resides in each one of us. The Guru or the Master takes each one to Her. These are the two eternal truths. But for this to happen, the first step is to want to take this inward journey more than anything else. Then leave all to the Guru and the Goddess.'

I have rambled on a bit through these chapters that you have, for want of better things to do or pure unadulterated desperation, decided to read. If a sentence, a phrase or a word makes sense and helps you to go within and embrace that Divine Spark, which enables you to move towards the Eternal Flame, it would be because you took that first step towards going back to the Source. A place where eventually all of us would not only reside within The One but also maybe realize that we all are one. But all this starts with the first step, which is with the belief that the True One resides within each one of us and is waiting for each one to start the divine communication.

It reminds me of this sage who once told another sage, 'We are stuck on this darn freezing mountain top without food, water, smoke and worst of all, the blasted phone charger. Now the only way to survive is to follow all the hogwash we have been preaching about connecting with the God and Goddess within, and hope that somebody up there or within us can hear our cry for help.'

Be blessed always.

1

The Guru Gone Wrong

A large number of people who come for channelling have similar stories to narrate. Each one has their Guru. These Gurus have various powers, and have a multitude of devotees whose faith in them has been unshaken for years.

Then something happens. Either the media reports a scandal or there is disillusionment after a personal interaction with the Guru.

Their faith is shaken. The one who they believed was a man or woman of God shatters their conviction and they realize that their Guru has feet of clay. It is a heart-wrenching phase for the individual whose faith now lies broken under the feet of reality.

But the ancient scriptures and even the Perfect Masters have made it clear that the Guru can never be wrong. The illusive Creator, who has in impulsive rashness created a world that makes no sense, plays a harp that needs immediate tuning and smokes questionable herbs somewhere in the ether, cannot be reached without the grace and guidance of a Guru.

But the truth is that the Guru has feet of clay. Forget being introduced to the Big Boy up there, the Guru seems to have gotten lost in the by-lanes of maya. Rumours or media reports indicate sex, havala and various scams linked to the Guru, the same person who was your be-all and end-all—your ticket to nirvana.

Then why have the scriptures discussed at length about the Guru and the need to hang on to every word of His for eternal salvation?

I write this as in the past six months I have met too many disillusioned people who have not only disowned their Gurus but also seem to have turned their back on our seemingly out-of-tune Harpist.

I keep elaborating on the difference between a Perfect Master and a Guide.

A Perfect Master is one who has merged with the Creator but still inhabits a physical shell to take on the sufferings of His/Her devotees and disciples, and helps them move forward towards self-realization.

The Perfect Master might or might not display a range of sparkling miracles, but the main plan of action is to evoke love, compassion and bring forth self-realization in each and every devotee and disciple who is under His wings.

The Master might initially fulfil the material, emotional and intellectual needs of the devotee to bring forth faith, and through faith, greater love and devotion. When the Master is convinced that the feet of the devotee are firmly entrenched on the path, then the beautiful yet painful process of karmic cleansing is initiated. But as the devotee is enveloped in love and faith, the process is borne with calmness. Thus the individual drops the baggage and slowly sheds various karmic attires, and stands completely bare, with nothing hindering his/her self-realization.

The path is rough but the devotee knows that he/she is never alone and it might take one full lifetime or more; the journey continues till it leads to the final destination. We finally reach the front-row seat in the hall where our Harpist performs the greatest gig of all times in a haze. One is brought on to the stage and then the individual realizes that not only is he/she the Harpist, the harp, the stage and the audience, but also everything and anything that ever has, is and will be created.

Thus the Perfect Master's sole purpose is to make each one of us realize our Godhood, or as one sage told another, to make us realize our damned selves.

The way the Perfect Master helps us through this metamorphosis could be through chanting, meditation and prayers, leading to love, compassion and phenomenal karmic cleansing, but the aim is to realize one's true higher self; to help the caterpillar *atma* evolve into the butterfly *Paramatma*. All caterpillars don't metamorphose into butterflies, but it is still a work in progress and the Perfect Master never lets go. Like a dedicated dhobi, the Master keeps at it till either the dirt from the cloth is removed or the cloth itself disappears.

What these dashing, often peculiar Dhobis really achieve is to make you realize the Guru within you—your higher self itself is the Guru, as the higher self is one with the Harpist and the strange off-key song that comes through is in reality the only song worth playing.

The problem is that we have begun to look at everybody as Perfect Masters. We have clubbed the Perfect Masters, sages, pirs, walis, *aulias*, *avdhoots*, *aghoris*, saints, mystics, lamas and Sufis with those who are mere guides and teachers (flawed just like you and me), and given them the stature of Godhood.

The one who dispels darkness is a Guru, but that individual is a Guru only for that particular moment, when consciously or by default, he/she lights a spiritual candle and with its soft glow, darkness is dispelled.

You, me or the dog on the street can dispel darkness, light the candle and play the role of the Guru for a short span, which in reality is the role of a guide. But you or me could be on the verge of breaking down as a result of our flaws, weaknesses and a dwindling bank balance. We are all Gurus and seekers every moment of our lives. That doesn't make us The Guru or the one free of weaknesses.

If you are following such an individual, who is himself/herself meandering in the by-lanes of illusion and karmic cleansing, eventually you are going to get your heart broken.

How would we know if the chap with that silly grin on his/her face is The One or not? How can one know who is a true Guru?

Well, the answer is simple. Does the Master make you a better human being, a more compassionate individual and a less judgemental person? Does he/she equip you to handle the recurrent karmic cleansing, guiding you towards the realization that we all are One and that only Oneness is real? And most importantly, does the Master make you realize your true self, without making you fearful of a false angry God and a hell that's slightly worse than dealing with cops, doctors, lawyers and often the in-laws?

A true Guru will tell you to go within and find your true self, and will make you focus not on Himself/Herself but in the Godhood within. When you start focusing on the God within the Master, even if the Master is not completely without human frailties, the chances of you being fooled, led astray or disillusioned is highly unlikely.

I have known individuals who I consider Masters and I am aware of their flaws. But, these individuals are still truly evolved and I seek that evolvement, and with my eyes open to their flaws, I love them.

When you go beyond the words and the physical charisma, and focus on the Godhood within a person—leave aside a Master or one who is still on the path—trust me, the individual, knowingly or unknowingly, will help you on the path of spirituality. This is possible even if you were to focus on the Godhood in a truly messed up individual.

The Master may not be without quirks and idiosyncrasies but the important thing to ask is whether the Master is without any dirt within, without a selfish agenda and has your well-being on the top of His/Her mind. A true Master will make you a better and a more compassionate human being first.

We are flawed. We come from either apes or the couple who walked about naked, eating that ill-fated apple. But within us is that spark. We can't go wrong if we follow the tune that comes from the questionable harp, played by the great Harpist Himself. The Master makes you hear that tune and urges you to go within as the music emanates from within your very depth.

With great power comes great responsibility, so go within as all that you seek is already there, waiting for you to open your eyes.

> *A true Guru will tell you to go within and find your true self, and will make you focus not on Himself/Herself but in the Godhood within.*
>
> *The Perfect Master might or might not display a range of sparkling miracles but the main plan of action is to evoke love, compassion and bring forth self-realization in each and every devotee and disciple who is under His wings.*

2

Burning the True Fire Within

I have family and friends who have suffered tremendously at the hands of fake Gurus, psychics and power-hungry astrologers.

What I have realized is that all of them have one thing in common: they all play the fear card.

I am aware that most religious books talk about greed, sloth, lust, envy, hate and slander as the greatest enemies of one's spiritual growth and self-realization. I am sure these emotions rot the soul. But according to me, the worst of the lot, the most underrated but the worst crippler of the soul, is fear.

Unfortunately, a number of these so-called Gurus and mediums nowadays use fear as the raw material to make certain their disciples become more dependent and less free.

From my minimal experience in the world of spirituality, I have come to the conclusion that the more power you give to somebody else, the weaker you truly get. Spirituality and spiritual growth are to be sought within oneself and not outside.

The more you externalize, the more impotent you become spiritually and the more you go within, deeper and deeper into the abyss of your very being, becoming one with your breath, you realize that everything is within; all the knowledge, power, wisdom and strength repose within each one of us.

But like the musk deer in search of the beautiful fragrance which emanates from it, we spend a lifetime trying to find the source of the enchanting fragrance, not realizing that it emanates from within us.

Fake Gurus, mediums and astrologers play the fear card, making you hand over your power to them and then you are dependent on them for the rest of your life.

Anybody who instils fear within you cannot be a true Guru. Anybody who sets you free is worth conferring and sharing your problems with. The one who sets you free of fear, superstition, the future, the planets, black magic and the evil eye is your friend, but the one who gives you back your power and shows you the path to the Harpist is your greatest well-wisher and Guru.

Look at the way we pray. Either it is like a business deal, where all we do is repeatedly ask for what we want or it is because we are fearful of something going wrong in our lives.

Baba Sai of Shirdi has so often told countless people that true prayer is one of gratitude and filled with love.

I would hate it if one of my three children were to love me out of fear. I would rather they not love me than do so. I hope that every time they hugged or expressed their love for me, it was not to get something in return. That would be a sad day for any parent or any lover or anybody who truly loves.

I have noticed that most people pray out of fear, out of habit or to get something from the Harpist. How many of us pray because we love Him? How many of us have prayed because we truly miss Him/Her? Because we feel incomplete without one's God, Goddess or Guru? How many of us have prayed just because it connects us to His/Her energy, divinity, love, radiance and Oneness?

When we pray, there should only be true love and gratitude in our minds. Nothing else. If there is anything else, worst of all fear, I wonder whether we are appeasing the Lord or pissing the old chap off. The day we pray in complete and pure love, I truly believe we shall light the fire within, which will burn away the malefic effects of planets, black magic and everything that doesn't come from Divine Radiance, as nothing can pollute the fire—all that goes into it becomes a part of it.

I have time and again met so many people who have gone into a shell as they have been filled with fear. Fear of the planets. Fear of astrological predictions. Fear of black magic or *nazar*, the evil eye. Fear of this and that. They have been made to do stuff ranging from the ludicrous to the senile, so that whatever plagues the person is taken care of. Yes, but after that is done, there are three others waiting in line to once again torment your peace of mind and ravage your very being.

Why is it that the one you have faith in doesn't fill you up with fearlessness and complete faith in The One, so that nothing ever truly destroys your sanity and makes you shiver with fear?

The festival of Holi is about burning away all the evil—all that stands in your way of radiance. But unfortunately, we end up celebrating all that is external. Take a few logs of wood, light a fire and watch it burning to ashes.

The story of Holi teaches us to nurture faith and devotion, so that one can never be touched by any external nonsense. There is no fire that can burn the one who truly loves, as he/she is then beyond the external and reposes in the true internal self—true internal self can't be harmed.

So the story goes that there was a chap called Mr Hiranyakashyap (henceforth called Mr H) who appeases Lord Shiva into granting him a boon. Lord Shiva, in His innocence, grants him a boon that he will not be killed by any man, animal or weapon anywhere, neither in the day nor at night.

After being granted the boon, Mr H goes nuts. He creates hell for all and proclaims that he is greater than all the three Gods, who seem to be scratching Their pious heads wondering why time and again They go about granting boons to neurotics and psychotics.

Mr H has a son called Prahlad, who truly loves Lord Vishnu. When Mr H tells his son to worship him as God, Prahlad pays no heed to him, as for him, his God is Lord Vishnu.

He is aware that his father is so filled with pride and hate that he will go to any lengths, including killing him. But for him, Lord Vishnu is God and Master, and the be-all and end-all of his existence. He is aware that his father will kill him, but he doesn't ask to be saved. He doesn't wait for any miracle to happen. He just loves Lord Vishnu and can't think beyond Him.

The fact is this: if you love your God, Goddess or Master, then you aren't waiting for Them to prove Themselves. Your faith isn't some test for Them. Scores of true lovers of The One have perished in their love for Him/Her.

The Harpist hasn't come down to save His lovers. The question you have to ask yourselves is do you love The One because you love Him/Her, or do you love The One because you want Him/Her to be at your beck and call and perform miracles, and make your life free of all strife and problems?

God is not a cosmic waiter at our beck and call. Either you love Him or you want to get into a business deal with Him. Trust me, nobody has profited from doing business with the Harpist. The chap is not a very good businessman.

So, Mr H tries various ways to force Prahlad to worship him and denounce Lord Vishnu. Prahlad disagrees. Mr H tries to kill Prahlad and Lord Vishnu saves him.

Please understand that we have got the plot wrong. We celebrate Holi not because Prahlad got saved by Lord Vishnu, but because Prahlad truly loved Lord Vishnu. His getting saved is merely ancillary. In the fire of true love and devotion, all that which is false is burnt away.

Mr H then calls his sister Holika, who too was granted a boon by one of the three Gods that she would never get burnt or killed by fire.

Holika sits on a burning pyre with the young Prahlad. Mr H is now certain that the brat would be annihilated, but to his shock, Prahlad escapes out of the fire unharmed, and Holika gets cooked good and proper.

Thus goes the legend of Holi.

The true legend is that love conquers all. That true love goes beyond the body, the planets, all the hocus-pocus and takes one to the Harpist, who goes about oblivious to one and all, playing His completely out-of-tune harp.

Holi is the burning of the internal fire that is meant to destroy everything that is impure or off the path and create a Divine Radiance—the Oneness which merges with The One.

Anything and anybody who tries to take you away from the path, true selfless love and joy, the freedom of fear and superstition and your true self, like Mr H and his sister, has to be avoided.

Go within. Just as Prahlad's love for Lord Vishnu was unconditional, without any business agenda or personal desire, I pray that we too are filled with such innocent love, the fragrance of which envelopes all of Creation, but first of all our very self.

Baba Sai of Shirdi loved to say during channelling, 'Your faith and love should be such that it shakes the very foundations of your God, Goddess and Guru.'

I pray that we are blessed with such faith and love, the kind that seeks nothing but a sigh and a smile from The One.

Be blessed.

The worst crippler of the soul is the emotion of fear.

The more power you give to somebody else, the weaker you truly get. Spirituality and spiritual growth are to be sought within oneself and not outside.

The one who sets you free of fear, superstition, the future, the planets, the black magic or the evil eye is your friend, but the one who gives you back your power and shows you the path to the Harpist is your greatest well-wisher and Guru.

Holi is the burning of the internal fire that is meant to destroy everything that is impure or off the path and create a Divine Radiance—the Oneness which merges with The One.

3

The Father, the Son, but Who Is the Holy Spirit?

I got an invite to write for *Speaking Tree* on a Good Friday and my first article appeared on Easter. For me, it has been a humbling experience and I hope my ramblings have given you some joy and hope; and not a perpetual migraine.

Most of the people who know of Lord Christ and Mother Mary have heard the sentence, 'In the name of the Father, the Son and the Holy Spirit.'

So who is this Holy Spirit?

We have the Creator . . . who is called the Father.

Then we have the Son . . . Jesus Christ and also all the Masters who are filled with the Christ Energy.

Now who exactly is the Holy Spirit?

According to me, the Holy Spirit is the Goddess Energy.

Thus, you have the Creator (Father Energy), the Son (the Christ or the Guru Energy) and then the Goddess (the Holy Spirit Energy, the Mother Energy).

Lord Shiv Himself has said that without the Goddess Energy called Shakti, He is just *shav* (a lifeless body).

The Holy Spirit is Shakti or Goddess Energy or Life Energy.

Without the Holy Spirit or Shakti, both God and Father as well as Son and Christ Energy are dormant energies. It is only the Goddess Energy or the Mother Energy or the Holy Spirit that drives the engine of Creation.

Without the Holy Spirit, you are dormant.

The Holy Spirit is the very life force that cruises through every aspect of Creation. From a sapling to a Perfect Master, it is the Divine Holy Spirit that gives life and takes us through the various stages of evolution and involution of consciousness.

God is the chief executive officer (CEO) who sits in radiance and divinity, but Shakti is the one who carries this radiance, divinity and fragrance to each living organism; the life force is the Goddess Energy. He has created the basic memorandum of understanding but it is the Goddess who implements it. However, like a loving mother, She wants no credit. So the Son is filled with Her Energy and it is with the Christ Energy that the Perfect Masters, along with the Archangels and Angels, run the show.

A grand production gone hilariously wrong as the entire cast is mankind.

So when you chant, 'In the name of the Father, the Son and the Holy Spirit', you are calling upon the entire family—Dad, Son and Mommy.

Baba Sai of Shirdi called his personal residence, a dilapidated mosque, Dwarka Mai.

Mai means mother.

He called the Holy Ash, which he distributed from the Holy Fire that has been burning in Dwarka Mai for more than 150 years, Dhuni Mai—the mother again.

Why would Baba Sai call a mosque and the Holy Fire a mother?

He sat in the mosque but without the Holy Energy and the Holy Spirit, even he—my sweetheart, my king, my Baba Sai of Shirdi—would only be shav . . . just the body. It is the divinity that passed through each cell within him that made him the Powerhouse, the Giant of Giants, the King of all Masters and the Rock Star with a chillum, who he truly was.

So it is all about the Holy Spirit and the Goddess Energy, and thus 'the Father, the Son and the Holy Spirit'.

A number of religions have downplayed the role of the Goddess Energy.

Zoroastrianism, Judaism, Christianity and Islam, to name a few, but the fact remains that if God is the Father and Christ is the Son, then there has to be a Mother, and the Holy Spirit is the Mother Energy.

Mother Mary didn't need Father Joseph to conceive Jesus, but the Lord needed Mother Mary to bring forth His Son, Jesus the Christ, to save us —the suffering and constipated mankind.

The resurrection of Jesus the Christ refers to the Holy Spirit, the Goddess Energy, the Mother Energy, the Chi and the Prana returning to Jesus's body and filling Him with the Christ Energy. What is the Christ Energy? A beautiful combination of the Father and Mother Energy or according to me, the Divine Energy or Shakti. So Jesus the Christ is the one filled with Shakti/the Holy Spirit/the Divine Energy.

Easter is the time when the Holy Spirit (Goddess Energy) filled the lifeless body of Jesus with Her Energy—the Christ Energy—or the Divine Life Spark which hails the glory of the Father, the Creator.

The Father, the Son and the Holy Spirit form the Holy Trinity.

The Holy Trinity that every religion talks about is Dad, Mom and a very enlightened *Bachha*.

I am sure scholars and learned spiritual people will have another take on this, but this is my view and by now, you, my dear friend, are sort of used to my ramblings.

I know that the standard stuff spoken about the Holy Trinity is that it is the Father who generates, the Son who is begotten, and the Holy Spirit who proceeds . . .

But my take is that the moment you have the Father and the Son . . . you have to have the Mother. You can't have Dad and Son without Mom.

The Father who generates (creates), the Son who is begotten (who comes down in flesh to show the way) and the Holy Spirit who proceeds (moves . . . in this case makes things move . . . means energizes stuff to move . . . means life spark . . . means Shakti . . . means Mother).

Even the way the sign of the cross is made by those in prayer signifies the Father, the Son and the Holy Spirit. Usually, one mentions the Father when the right hand touches the forehead, the Son when one touches the heart, Holy when the left shoulder is touched and Spirit when the right shoulder is touched (it seems Eastern Christians touch the right shoulder first and then left, but that's immaterial).

So one starts off with the name of the Father by touching the forehead . . . more importantly, the Third-Eye Chakra. The head stands for thought, word and intellect, usually associated with the Male Energy.

Then one touches the heart with the word Son. The region of the heart is associated with the Heart Chakra—selfless love and compassion—extremely important for Masters and those filled with the Christ or Krishna Energy working in the physical plane.

Then comes Holy on the left shoulder and Spirit on the right shoulder. The fingers pass over the heart while touching each shoulder. The Holy Spirit or the Mother protects her Son from everything, embracing and nurturing her Son.

Once again, this is my two-bit understanding.

When the Kundalini Energy or the Divine Energy rises from the Base Chakra right up to the Crown Chakra, it charges one with divine knowledge and power. This is called the Divine Mother Energy, Shakti or Christ Energy, which is the ignited Divine Energy that makes you realize Godhood within oneself.

The laptop I work on can be the male energy, the idiot typing this blog can be the conveyor or the one who gets the message across, but both the laptop and the idiot, without power, can only best twiddle their toes. Without power or energy or electricity or battery or Shakti, the laptop is just a very expensive device to protect oneself with when the wife goes nuts and begins to throw stuff at you from the kitchen. It is the power that starts the machine and then the energy and inspiration comes about to write it (energy and inspiration is once again a life spark, the Holy Spirit).

I know there are various explanations. I have written my reality. It may make sense to you or you might think I have lost the plot. No matter what you think, you must realize that the yin and yang energy that exists in every human has to run through Creation. It is the positive and negative that propels things forward and thus there has to be male and female energy in the cosmos.

We are after all created in the image of the Lord . . . *Ardhanarishwara*, the androgynous form of Lord Shiva and Maa Parvati . . . or how I believe the good God/Goddess is, our Father and Mother, as one Energy. Thus, 'In the name of the Father, the Son and the Holy Spirit.'

Be blessed.

> *Without the Holy Spirit or Shakti, both God and Father as well as Son and Christ Energy are dormant energies. It is only the Goddess Energy or Mother Energy or the Holy Spirit that drives the engine of Creation.*
>
> *When the Kundalini Energy or the Divine Energy rises from the Base Chakra right up to the Crown Chakra, it charges one with divine knowledge and power. This is called the Divine Mother Energy, Shakti or Christ Energy, which is the ignited Divine Energy that makes you realize Godhood within oneself.*

4

The Amen Philosophy

Igrew up with my maternal grandmother. We seven cousins lived with her and our lives were filled with fun and joy. Then one day she left her cute doll-like physical frame. I not only miss her more with each passing day but yearn for those days of living with my brothers and sisters, cocooned in the womb of happiness and laughter. Each day was a celebration.

There were a few things my grandmother spoke about that made no sense to me when I was a kid. I would scratch my head and tell her, 'Granny, you are so funny!' But now all that she told me or blessed me with makes so much sense that it brings an ache to my rather battered heart. I will write about one such philosophy which she tried to constantly hammer into my thick, fat head.

She would always tell me, 'Remember, always think positively—think good thoughts, speak good words and always wish well for others as God says "Amen" only once a day. We don't know when He/She says Amen. So you need to be always careful bachha.'

And I remember asking her, 'But why does He/She say Amen just once and why in heaven does He/She not have a fixed time to say Amen?'

And she would laugh, her tummy going up and down, and tell me, 'Oh my boy, promise me you will never become an adult in your heart; always remain a child at heart.'

Now when I look back, I realize that she was so wise. She instilled or at least tried to instil within me the power of thought, intention and word. I remember wondering when the Big Boss would wake up from His heavily smoke-induced trance, clear the throat and say, 'Amen'. Thus, I tried my level best to shy away from negative thoughts, angry reflections, hurtful deliberations and self-destructive as well as pessimistic silent ramblings, all because I did not want to create issues for either myself or anybody around me.

This simple Amen philosophy has also helped me become less judgemental (I hope) of all the idiots who drive vehicles on our roads and the so-called leaders who threaten to govern us and the world at large. I say, 'Let it be, who knows when the Big Boss is going to wake up and say the darn word.'

The philosophy is simple, but if we realize the true purpose of the Amen philosophy, It can make a tremendous difference to our quality of life—emotional, mental and physical, but mainly spiritual. When you truly understand the essence of this sweet grandmother ideology, of staying on the path of positivity and wishing well for one and all, it makes spirituality truly innocent and beautiful. Well at least it put everything in perspective for me. If I had to choose between all the spiritual books on one side and this simple philosophy on the other, I would choose to go with this noble four-letter word.

I have so often thanked my Lord and Master Baba Sai for not fulfilling certain wishes or whims of mine and for doing exactly what He/She wanted, despite my fervent longings, and not getting up and saying aloud 'Amen'. So often, grace comes in the form of a rejection slip.

I remember once I was upset with a friend and in a fit of anger, told him a lot of things I should not have. A few days later, his father informed me that my friend had died, all of a sudden, due to a heart attack. He was just twenty-seven. It has been over twenty years, but I still cringe at remembering my words and anger, and even now hope and pray that the Amen word wasn't uttered then by a seemingly distant Lord.

We have been told by Masters that the word came first. The word certainly came first, but could not have preceded the thought, unless God does not think before speaking, which I hope is not true. I am certain a lot of thought went first before the word, but it goes to show how important our thoughts and words are in the larger scheme of things. Thoughts and words have their own power. So it is little wonder that Prophet Zarathustra based the doctrine of Zoroastrianism on good thoughts, good words and good deeds.

If you think about good things, you will speak good things and eventually do good. The Dalai Lama has mentioned somewhere that lifetimes of good karma can be wiped away by a single destructive thought and word. This is how important our thoughts and words are, and most often we give importance to everything but these two crucial aspects of our lives.

The breath determines one's thoughts. Thoughts influence our words. The breath, thoughts and words become fuel for our deeds. Thus, it all originates from breath and leads to deeds, which eventually germinate into karma and becomes all-pervading as one's destiny. You do not become what you eat, you become what you think and may be this is why our elders spun such simple but deeply spiritual narratives to sow within our fertile consciousness the foundations of deep-rooted spirituality.

When I look around me, the mess we have created of our planet and our own spiritual journey, and the utter rubbish going on in the name of God, is sad and heartbreaking. If God has taken shelter in His/Her own sanctuary of eternal bliss, it must be because the Creator's heart too must be broken seeing the way we go about life and our perpetual disregard for goodness and decency. After seeing the ruthlessness of people around and the senseless tragedies and inconsolable sadness that prevail everywhere, I have begun to feel my grandmother was right—the Old Man wakes up just once a day to say Amen and then goes back to sleep. God is in heaven and is fast asleep.

Thus, I would suggest that it is all the more imperative for our own sanity and peace that we be careful of what we think, either of ourselves or those around us. Be very vigilant of what you wish for my friend, for God forbid, your wish may be granted and you might not be able to forgive yourself. Sometimes one's fulfilment of prayer might prevent the karmic onslaught waiting to be unleashed.

Be careful as truly, the less we go within, the more we are in danger of being pulverized by our free will gone wrong. Go within, as within resides The One, waiting and aching for you and me to finally embrace the only reality—the reality that everything is one big tamasha, one elaborated play gone horribly wrong, and the only reality is that of Oneness and going back Home.

Be blessed always.

Lifetimes of good karma can be wiped away by a single destructive thought and word. This is how important our thoughts and words are, and most often we give importance to everything but these two crucial aspects of our lives.

You do not become what you eat, you become what you think.

Staying on the path of positivity and wishing well for one and all makes spirituality truly innocent and beautiful.

So often, grace comes in the form of a rejection slip.

5

The Most Powerful Blessing

Before I begin writing about the most powerful blessing, prayer and state of being, let me do a bit of rambling first. I assure you, in a very warped way, that this incoherent monologue is sort of connected with the main theme.

I have often wondered as to why I was parcelled off to a boarding school in Panchgani when I was just six years of age. On and off, I have had a few glimpses of my early years. All through my life, I have had this faint memory of my school bus being taken to a police station. Then to the hospital. The next day, I would have dinner in a very well-kept home. The memories of all three incidents would keep resurfacing.

Then a shut cupboard. In the luggage compartment of a car. Lot of commotion outside.

I would nod my head, wonder and then go on to make a hash of whatever I was doing.

Last month, I had gone to visit my Godmother who stays two hours away from Pune. I call her Aai, which in Marathi language means mother. She used to come to sweep at my maternal grandmother's place. My mom, who was then pregnant with me, liked the young, hardy woman and it was decided henceforth that she would live and work at my grandmother's place. Once I came out, yelling and screaming, her life revolved around me. Thus, I call her Aai and for her, I can do no wrong. God can go ahead and try to make her see that I should have been strangulated at birth, but for her, I am beyond reproach.

I meet her once every few months. That day, for some odd reason, I spoke about the visions of the police station, the hospital, the cupboard, etc. and she smiled and proudly told me and my friends about it all.

Well it seems when I was not yet six years of age, I had got into a fight with another boy or a group of boys in the school bus. The fight was rather ugly and none of us boys would give up, so eventually the bus had to be taken to the police station, where the cops separated us. The hospital vision was a follow-up to the police station. One of the boys was badly injured; I was hurt too. So late at night, our parents arrived to see their children, five-and-a-half-year-old or slightly older, sitting on plastic chairs, with bandages all over their body, and two cops snoring away to glory. The dinner followed the next day as one of the boys was badly injured; I felt my parents were waving a white flag to compensate for the strange behaviour of their son. Of course, there were no doubts that I must have been at fault because just a month before, I had hidden myself in the boot of Dr Gandhi's Ambassador or Fiat, while the entire school searched for me. The cops were called and an official complaint of kidnapping was going to be filed, when I came out of my hiding space, grinning, and ran for dear life.

The cupboard scene happened a few years before this event. I had hidden myself in a cupboard and my poor maternal grandmother had to eventually call the cops. They then heard some knocking from the cupboard and voila, I came out and asked for some food as I was hungry.

So I was packed off to Billimoria High School, Panchgani. I was told I was being sent for a picnic. We all got out of the bus. I looked around. I asked my cousin brother, Viraf, when we were going to return home. He smiled and said, 'Six months later.' I said, 'Jolly good.' A few minutes later, Rohit Bachkaniwalla and I got involved in a fist fight.

The usual complaint about me was that I was only interested in having a good laugh, playing and raising Cain. Every teacher would religiously tell my parents through letters and personal meetings that they all loved me, but I was always up to mischief.

Hence, I could never understand why my maternal grandmother and my dad's dad would always bless me saying, *'Hasto–khelto reh'*, which in English means: 'Always remain and be joyful and playful.'

I would scratch my head and say, 'Ok, for sure', and then take their blessings literally. All I would do was to have a great time, playing, laughing, climbing trees and mountains, and doing stuff which, if Providence had an iota of common sense, would have made me leave my mortal, battered body.

Then my teachers and family would give me grief. I got tired of being blessed with one thing and having to deal with chaos and long-drawn lectures for living up to it.

So one day I looked at my grandmother in the eye and I told her, 'Make up your mind, either you want me to be always happy, joyous and playful, or you want me to become like all those sensible, boring children who listen to everything everybody tells them to do.'

I remember my grandmother chuckling, with her tummy going up and down. She wiped the tears from her eyes, looked at me and said, 'What will you do once I am dead and gone? I worry for you.' I told her to stick to the main issue of either blessing me with something sensible that did not get me into trouble or standing up for me when the boring world threw tantrums at me for being mischievous.

'You have made a lot of people angry by latching the doors of the houses in the colony while people were sleeping . . .'

'That damn milkman saw me, didn't he? The same chap who keeps adding water to the milk. He would do it tomorrow too . . .'

'As for my blessing, you shall know its true worth when you grow up and have a family of your own or may be when I am gone to Sai.'

Nearly four decades later, I remember her words and most importantly, cherish her blessings. A lot of us are blessed with or bless others with stuff like, 'long life', 'healthy life' or 'prosperous life'. The strangest of all blessings to women is, 'May you never be a widow in your life', which means, 'May you die before your hubby cops it.'

I have been blessed to become enlightened, have my Chakras opened and what not. I always wonder who in their right mind would want all these strange blessings.

All I want is to be happy and take every blow, all the ups and downs, and whatever life, fate and karma have in store for me, gracefully, joyously and playfully. Growing old is mandatory and boring. Growing up is optional. Stick to the latter. Adults are boring because we no longer have joy and playfulness in our lives. Our priorities have changed. We have become exactly who we as kids would dread and make fun of. Boring. Intellectual. Judgemental. Ungrateful. Stupid adults.

You know what? I have realized that a healthy, long and prosperous life mean nothing if there is no joy, laughter and playfulness in one's life.

One can have everything, but without joy, laughter and mischief, life is like a five-course meal with no salt and spice, and no sugar in the sweet dish. Or like the story of a seeker who spent years risking his life to climb a ridiculously steep mountain, in order to hear one life-changing sentence from the sage who resides on top of the mountain. When the climber eventually reaches the top of the mountain, he sees a frail man, smoking something that in certain countries would get him into legal trouble, who says, 'Wrong mountain brother, that . . . sage sits on that one.'

Of course, now I have realized a greater depth to this blessing, '*Hastey–kheltey rehana*'.

We all are a byproduct of our karma. Now before I begin on karma, let us make one thing clear. You either do not believe in God or you believe in a just God. A God who takes no sides. A God who is reasonable. Thus if you believe in a just God, then you have to believe in the laws of cause and effect or karma.

Karma is the ramifications of our free will used in this lifetime or past lives, which catches up with us. The karmic bill has to be paid. Lord Vishnu had to manifest as Lord Rama as He too could not escape the laws of karma. If He had to come down on the physical plane to pay this karmic bill, what hope in heaven or hell do we have?

The laws of karma dictate that as you sow, so shall you reap. You can pray and lead as pious a life as you want to, so pious that your purity could give the Angels above an inferiority complex, but one cannot escape one's own karma. If your destiny and karmic blueprint necessitates you to have your nose rubbed into the ground, you can be sure that your nose will be rubbed into the ground.

If your karmic blueprint does not include financial success, my dear psychotic friend, you can be rest assured that you will be in financial want through this particular lifetime. Remember, I am not trying to advocate fatalism. Far from it. Yes, our duty is to give life and every moment our very best, but one needs to realize that eventually, the result, be it success or failure, is not in our control. Thus, every religion and every Master preaches the need to do your best and be detached from the rest.

So now, if you are not destined for financial success, you can pray all you want, but financial gloom will follow you like a demented shadow.

One should rather pray to one's God, Goddess or Master like this: 'Oh *Upparwalla* (The wise one occupying the uppermost penthouse in evolution), I am not seeking anything. Though in reality I do seek a lot, I am doubtful of receiving any of that. So I am asking You for something which You can grant without going on and on about karma and the laws of destiny. This is what I ask of You—that I go through whatever life has in store for me with happiness, joy and even playfulness. You can grant me this as You are my be-all and end-all, and I am your messed-up child with a wreckful karma. Grant me this and then let the laws of karma deal with me, I have no issue.'

How can one's God, Goddess or Master not grant us this little childlike wish? We haven't asked for a change of the karmic manifesto, have we? No wealth. No progeny. No success. No fancy car. Nothing. Just something as understated as joy and playfulness. Most people do not even want all this. They want the big stuff—bliss, power, wealth and leadership. But fools like us want the underrated stuff like joy and laughter. So come on Lord, be a sport. You created us, but did we ask You to create us? No. You did. Thus technically, it is Your fault that we occupy this battered body and ravaged planet. So, the least that can be done for us is to bless us with joy, happiness, laughter and playfulness so that we can go through whatever is in store for us with a smile. Do this for us. Do this for all those who suffer. For all the kids and women raped, sold and killed. For all those suffering from illness, heartache, deceit, anger, hate, poverty and all the sorrow and helplessness. Yes, yes, yes . . . it is all our fault and we have to go through this life carrying the load of our karmic bullshit, but let us go through it 'hastey–kheltey'.

If everything is about sowing and reaping, I am sure it is more about realizing and learning from our mistakes. Atleast grant the blessing of joy and laughter to those who have realized and learnt from their mistakes or experiences or the wrong use of free will. That much can be done. This much can be prayed for by us all.

Eventually, I have realized that this simple blessing or prayer is all I want. Love thrives where there is peace and joy. Spirituality thrives when there is centredness. Life, in the body or in the spirit world, becomes a very heavy burden to carry without laughter and joy.

The problem with growing old is that you begin to miss the simple joys of childhood. In reality, what one misses is the simple emotion called joy.

Often when I look back, the only thing I truly miss is being filled with joy. The other stuff often seem to pale in comparison to what was once an inherent part of our nature.

If spirituality is to become all serious and boring, then I want nothing to do with it. But spirituality in reality is joyful. The Masters were filled with childlike joy and playfulness. It is we, the dwarfs, who are filled with our prejudices, judgemental attitude and our adult bullshit that has destroyed the very essence of spirituality and simple, joyous living.

So, if you want to bless somebody you love or even yourself, do not forget this hastey–kheltey rambling of a man who visited a police station at the age of five.

Be blessed.

> *One can have everything, but without joy, laughter and mischief, life is like a five-course meal, with no salt and spice, and no sugar in the sweet dish.*
>
> *Love thrives where there is peace and joy. Spirituality thrives when there is centeredness. Life, in the body or in the spirit world, becomes a very heavy burden to carry without laughter and joy.*
>
> *Spirituality in reality is joyful. The Masters were filled with childlike joy and playfulness.*

6

God Is in the Blasted Details Too

There are some who are spiritual. There are many who would like to believe they are spiritual. Between these two sects the common man very often gets mauled. The problem is it is rather difficult to differentiate between a truly spiritual person and the idiot who professes to be one. Both look alike, behave in a similar way and talk the same spiritual gibberish—very often mouthing strange words that make little sense to common folk like us, who are desperately trying to keep body and soul together.

So, when talking about the larger scheme of things like lust, wrath, sloth and theft, both the truly spiritual and the absurdly counterfeit walk and talk the same language. It's hard to differentiate the corn from the chaff, and the worst part of it all is that the pseudo kind is not very often putting on an act.

It is mainly when you go deep that one realizes the difference between the chap who is spiritual and the sap who would like to believe that he/she is spiritual.

First and foremost, what does being spiritual truly mean? According to me, and trust me, I have been wrong so many times that there should be a new word created just to define my idiosyncrasies, being spiritual means to operate from the Oneness of the spirit.

And what does operating from the Oneness of the spirit mean? Well, when one lives with the complete belief and conviction that each one of us—every living organism that throbs with life—has come forth from The One and thus Oneness rules, then one begins to operate from the spirit.

The answer to why the Great One decided to self-create and worse, go about creating mankind, is one I am certain the Great One is not going to be able to convincingly provide. He/She has really messed up here, but I don't want to drive myself round the twist, wondering why somebody in the stature of God could do something so slow-witted as to go about creating mankind and then put us through His/Her laws of karma and all the goofy stuff. So, we shall proceed with the other stuff worth rambling about.

Thus for me, each one of us has gushed forth like a spark from the Great Fire, and thus each one has the Great Fire cruising through our very soul. If we have come forth from the Great Fire, each spark has embodied within itself the Great Fire. Therefore, the Great Fire has the same DNA as the confused spark and thus they are One.

So for me, spirituality means Oneness and when you operate from the spirit, never forgetting that eventually only Oneness is true and everything that creates shadows and duality are false, then I would like to believe that the individual has begun the walk on the spiritual path. Mouthing words of wisdom thus need not qualify you as a spiritual person in my vision; if you are operating from duality and not Oneness, then there is something within you that doesn't have the larger good of all Creation, past, present and future in mind. When you operate from Oneness, you have in a second put your faith in The One and all that which He/She stands for.

Thus, first and foremost, a truly spiritual person, according to me, understands this essence of Oneness and begins to operate from the Spirit and not from the tangible body or physical elements that surrounds one.

Now when you operate knowing that only the Spirit is real and all else a mirage, then one's priorities too change and with the change in priorities comes forth compassion and largeness of heart.

A spiritual person is large of heart for the simple reason that He/She has realized the futility of possession and ownership, as both create duality and are transitory, while giving and sharing are the foundations of all that which is noble and divine.

Thus, according to me, all those who unify and share operate from the oasis of spiritualism and all those who divide and hoard operate from the abysses of duality and self-centredness; wherever there exists just the self, there cannot exist a holistic environment of Oneness.

Now if you are still awake, let us proceed to the tangible stuff where the true essence of spirituality lies. I have realized these are in the little things that subtly show you whether you do walk the talk and whether the walk is taking you up to the zenith or into the valley, through various confusing by-lanes, into the bowels of hell.

The problem is that most of us have been given the larger picture by our parents, our teachers and our so-called moralists, and the little things that equally matter have been waylaid on the path to The One.

We have been constantly told not to lie, not to steal and abstain from wrath and lust. Great. If you have been able to do all this, send me a mail on how you did it. Good for you. You are on the path. Big time.

But for me, the little stuff is equally important. On any given day, the number of times we abstain from gossip, slander, prejudices and forming judgements is equally important and it is in these little things, inconsequential to most people, where the real spirituality of an individual shines through.

Don't get me wrong. The big stuff is equally important.

We are a community of gossip mongers. We like to feel good about ourselves and the easiest way to do so is by putting somebody else down, through small talk or petty thoughts. Slandering someone else through action, thought or word is as wrongful as indulging in the 'big boys' of sin.

Time and again, Baba Sai of Shirdi as well as other Giants have commented on the pitfall of slander, gossip and backbiting. We need to take heed of it and realize that these little things are as important as the stuff written in commandments.

We have a tendency to put people down, pass comments on others, their way of life, thought, dress sense, speech, weight, lingo and yes, their flaws. In turn, we too are getting waylaid, losing focus, creating a sense of duality and thus straying from the path of Oneness.

The path of Oneness comes from compassion. Compassion comes from an understanding that each one of us is a strange blend of past-life karmas, DNA and upbringing. Thus, to judge somebody without understanding the combination and blend constituting each individual is not only unfair but prejudicial and childish. Hate and jealousy can be disguised in various layers of ignorance and very often, we indulge in the looseness of talk that takes us away from the higher peaks of spirituality into the abysses of pettiness and duality.

The path of Oneness is the path of taking one and all along with us, whether they think, act, speak, dress or conduct themselves like you do. Our issue is that we want everyone to confirm to our way of thought and life, and we feel whoever doesn't is wrong.

Spirituality means liberating oneself and others from darkness, and not being engulfed by the chains of prejudices and duality. Oneness does not mean each one of us should be alike, but that no matter the differences, we all are one as we have come forth from The One.

The moment we start judging, passing comments, putting somebody down by slander or backbiting, we are losing the plot. We have gone astray. Yes, we may not be indulging in the big stuff that all the books and our elders keep warning us to avoid, but we are still far away from the embrace of The One as we are spreading duality and not Oneness.

According to me, we can only merge when we are in the same state as when we ventured forth from The One. We were pure. When the strains of lust, wrath or the little stuff like gossip, slander and being judgemental stick to our aura, we are far away from the pristine state that we came forth from. Whatever keeps us away from merging will make us come back to work out our weaknesses. The more times we come back, the chances of us falling deeper into the mire of maya, and the ramifications of our free will, accumulated karma and other things only increase. Thus, be wary of the big stuff, but work on the so-called inconsequential things as eventually only a state of pure nothingness is going to take us back to our original state. It will be a crying shame if one is prevented from experiencing that state of Oneness over silly stuff like gossip, slander and backbiting.

Be blessed.

When one lives with the complete belief and conviction that each one of us—every living organism that throbs with life—has come forth from The One and thus Oneness rules, then one begins to operate from the Spirit.

All those who unify and share operate from the oasis of spiritualism and all those who divide and hoard operate from the abysses of duality and self-centredness.

Oneness does not mean each one of us should be alike, but it means no matter the differences we all are one as we have come forth from The One.

The path of Oneness is the path of taking one and all along with us, whether they think, act, speak, dress or conduct themselves like you do.

<h1 style="text-align:center">7</h1>

The Art of Creating Hell for Oneself

Whether we like it or not, we are being manipulated many times in a day. Whether we accept it or not, our thoughts, words and actions are manoeuvred many times in a day. Whether we want it or not, we hand over our power and peace of mind to be crushed or mishandled many times in a day.

The sad part of all this is that often, nobody is even aware that they are playing the role of the manipulator or being manipulated; enacting the alpha dog or the victim; handing over our power or becoming a tyrant.

Welcome to the art of creating hell for oneself. It is really simple in reality. Terribly and shamelessly natural. It comes from the self-inflicted survival instinct called the reflex philosophy.

There are certain physical points in the body which, if touched at the right place with the right force, brings forth an involuntary and an automatic spontaneous response. The individual is not even part of the responses.

If you caress a dog at a certain place, the quadruped furball's leg will begin to shake. Of course, the wagging of the tail is not a reflex. It is from the heart. The reflex of the tail is embedded in the heart strings and when the heart misses a beat, the tail wags. When it experiences fear, the tail goes between the legs. None of this is a reflex action. But be it a friend or a foe, if someone touches or scratches a particular point on the dog's body, the poor mutt's leg will begin to tap-dance.

But I am not talking about the reflex action. I am talking about a very dangerous spontaneous response not associated with our body but worse, associated with our mind and our tongue, seeping into our heart, our consciousness and then into our very being.

If there is one thing that has the stamp of the Devil, then that is the soul-crippling, the sanity-obliterating, the happiness-annihilating . . . the self-destructive knack nurtured and enhanced by all human beings—to react rather than act.

Take a look at our lives. Contemplate or remember occasions where you have lost the plot; where you went against everything logical and rational; when you indulged in a manner that you would never ever expect of yourself; when from the pinnacle of self-respect you dived into the bowels of self-loathing. Nine out of ten times we would have concluded that if only we had handled the situation a little more calmly, maturely or just silently, things would have settled peacefully, with just a little dent to our self-respect, may be even to our advantage.

We react so often, so abruptly and so consistently that I wonder if there is a natural reactor safely tucked away in our body.

Please understand that there is a colossal difference between acting and reacting.

When one acts in a situation, one is in control of one's thoughts, words and actions. One initiates a proceeding where one has already thought of the ramifications and reactions, and knowing beforehand the consequences of the action, one is ready with plan B, and so forth.

Even if one acts in anger, the anger is in one's control and thus the anger fuels one's passion, determination and helps the rush of adrenaline to flow in a manner that enhances one's determination. The long and short of all this *bhashan* is that the one who initiates an action is in complete control of himself or herself.

So, one who initiates an action or one who acts does so by keeping the pros and cons, plausible ramifications and outcomes in mind, and then decides which particular action justifies whatever has to follow. You are the master of your thoughts, words and actions, and thus you are completely aware of the consequences. You might achieve your objective or you might not, but the chances of you falling flat on your face are rather limited.

Remember that when one acts, one uses all the senses and thus the chances of doing something phenomenally self-destructive are rather slim, as you have come forth from a place of calmness and centredness; whatever follows is going to be well thought of, even though success may not always be ensured. But the consolation is that I and only I am responsible for the consequences and if given another chance, in all probability, I would still go about this situation in the same manner.

But when one reacts, one is not in command of the situation. One is like a horny bull in a china shop. Various gaseous combustions happen in various openings in the anatomy.

When an individual reacts, he/she is not in control of his/her senses and as the action has not been well thought of, the ramification of one's reaction is also left to chance, very often, not accruing well for the individual. He/she is being controlled by his/her reaction and thus nine out of ten times, one has lost the battle and the war even before the first shot has been fired. When one reacts, one is consciously or unconsciously being manipulated by the other party while being led into the battlefield, with both arms tied at the back.

When we react, we have shut the door on calmness, centredness and common sense. With the three Cs kept out of the battle, you have as much chance to come out smelling of roses, as a yak has in solving a convoluted crossword puzzle.

This is because my reflex action is now either operating from my tongue or my fist, without the cooperation and assistance of my common sense, calm reasoning and silent deliberation. The worst part of it all is that I can be manipulated to react twenty times a day and the moment someone realizes this tendency of mine, I can be manipulated as many times in any given situation, without even realizing that I am making a buffoon of myself and my life.

We react countless times. Very often stepping on one landmine after another, as expected by the opposite party. The worst part of playing this game of reaction is that we become pawns in the game of life. Those close to us can manipulate us to think, talk and act the way they want.

It is like the one who acts has won half the battle over the one who reacts. Apart from making an idiot of oneself, one is bamboozled in front of our near and dear ones, time and again, through the process of reaction. Our sensitive emotional buttons are in the hands of those who can make us do eventually as they wish, and you may go through all this little realizing how badly you have been manoeuvred all your life, all because of the inability of not reacting. I know this might sound drastic, but trust me, there are innumerable people living their lives in a state of perpetual reaction.

Also understand that very often a person who only acts and does not react might appear to be reacting but the individual is operating from the space of having thought out the ifs, whys and whats of the situation. He/she has decided to still go ahead after contemplation, even if it means showcasing aggression and anger. Eventually, the individual has taken this step not as a reaction but as a planned initiative.

How does one slowly get out of the clutches of reaction? Well frankly, one needs to be in a state of constant awareness for that. It is like walking through a field of land mines. There are enough indications of landmines, all one needs to do is tread cautiously. If one does so, the chances of stepping on a landmine and indulging in the arithmetic of countless divisions can be avoided. For this, one has to be clearly in a state of calmness or be in the moment or be one with the breath, with the promise that, 'Thou shall not be violent, in thought, word or action, till one has counted slowly to twenty, and then through silent contemplation comes about one's next step of action.'

I know this is all a bit too much for us. We are so used to wearing boxing gloves that we might as well sleep with them attached to our body. But I still feel we are missing out on living a fulfilled life just because we insist on going through this process of reaction, followed by reacting to the reaction and so on.

If one does not want to be manipulated, then it is best to prevent oneself from falling in this quicksand of instant response. If you want to do something, it makes good sense to initiate that process rather than be manoeuvred into it.

The process of reaction can be controlled. No religious book may have mentioned it but trust me, this sickness of reacting to one and all has led more people down the path of damnation and grief compared to the usual so-called evils and sins that dot most pages of religious books.

If we have to go through grief and damnation, we might as well make sure we have initiated that process than be manipulated into making an ape out of ourselves.

Be blessed always.

If there is one thing that has the stamp of the very Devil, then that is the soul-crippling, the sanity-obliterating, the happiness-annihilating . . . the self-destructive knack nurtured and enhanced by all human beings—to react rather than act.

When one reacts, one is being consciously or unconsciously manipulated by the other party while being led into the battlefield, with both arms tied at the back.

If one does not want to be manipulated, then it is best to prevent oneself from falling in this quicksand of instant response. If you want to do something, it makes good sense to initiate that process rather than be manoeuvred into it.

8

Go beyond Perceptions and Expectations

The simple philosophy for a sane life is to not let somebody else's perceptions of you become your reality; no matter how hard you try, you are never going to meet and live up to the expectations of others.

If you can follow this two-pronged way of life, trust me, you will be saving yourself from serious grief and heartbreak.

Perceptions and expectations are the two least talked about causes of sadness and gloom. Once again, like reacting to situations, these two emotions encage most of us in their maze of darkness. We live our entire lives trying to live up to the expectations and perceptions of our near and dear ones, and the world at large, and fail miserably. The fact is that you can never live up to the perceptions and expectations of one and all.

I mean Gods, Goddesses and Gurus have not been able to live up to the perceptions and expectations of Their followers. Imagine, if They have not succeeded, then what chance do we poor, dimwit human beings have!

Look at our lives. Are we not all the time trying to match up to the perceptions and expectations of one and all? It starts from the family. One or both the parents wants a child to be encased in a certain personality, a career, a way of life, a way of belief or a way of diet. The grooming or brainwashing begins from there. A simple sentence like, 'My child is very obedient, he/she will never disobey me', is conditioning the child into believing that he/she is not supposed to speak out his/her mind to the parent as that would mean disobeying the parent. This means: 'This is not what we expected of you and you have let us down', which implies, 'Make my perception of who you are into your reality, no matter what.'

In fact, so often, two loved ones may have a completely different view of who you are and how you will handle each situation.

A simple example is that of a married man. The parents have a certain perception of their son, and they have various expectations based on their perceptions. The wife is going to have a different set of views about the same man. Very often, what may suit the parents might not suit the wife and vice versa. No matter how hard the individual tries to live up to either the parents' or his wife's expectations, he, very often, will not be able to make all those involved happy. Eventually, either the parents or the spouse is going to say, 'I did not expect this of you and you have let me down.' It happens to both men and women.

One thing is certain: the parents or spouse may get on with their demands, but for the man, it is a lose-lose situation, especially if the poor, daft man has tried to live up to everybody's perception and expectation of who he should be and how he should handle a situation.

The best part of it all is that as a parent, you want your son to behave in a certain manner, but as in-laws, you will want your daughter to be married to a man who uses his own brains and is not dictated by his parents.

The wife will want her husband to stand up to his parents, but the same wife will want her brother to obey their parents and not be influenced by his wife.

The game never ends. Use your bloody mind to find the sensible way out of a situation. But how many of us imbibe this simple way of life?

It is only when the man decides to live true to himself, irrespective of what the parents and the spouse think about him and the situation, will he be living his life—one filled with a sense of truth and calmness. Otherwise, he will either get a pat on his back for living up to somebody's belief or get kicked between the legs for letting somebody down.

Now get his kids, friends, colleagues and then the world involved too. How can one live up to so many different perceptions? What may make you an ideal child could make you a lousy spouse and a truly spineless parent. After a point, the individual begins to doubt himself/herself on every aspect. He/she begins to have no self-respect and then slowly moves into the abyss of darkness and negativity.

'This is not what I expected out of you' basically means, 'I have a leash around your neck, so when you feel the tug, do as I wish.' Being true to oneself is not easy. But very often, it is the only way to live if one wants to live a centred life.

But the fact is that we all are very often not living our lives, but the lives others want us to live.

So often, peer pressure is nothing but trying to live up to other's view of how we must dress, speak, behave and live. I have met so many parents, scared witless about how peer pressure affects or will affect their child. But instead of enforcing self-belief in the child, they are only scared of how the world will manipulate their child when very often, they themselves are leading the brigade of manipulation—on how they would want their child to live his/her life, how the child must behave with them and their society, what career to take, who and when to marry, and so on. One is either grappling with society or family.

It is only when an individual says, 'I will give my best and do what I feel is right in every given situation, irrespective of how you or the world perceives me and my actions to be', does an individual begin to lead his/her life, for the first very time. As parents, do we really give this freedom to our children?

Many years ago, I met Ramanand Sagar, the director and producer of the cult Ramayana series. One day, we were sitting and chatting in his beautiful home. He looked at me and said, 'Boss, you must be having a really hard time with the world.' He used to call me 'boss' for some reason. I had no idea whatsoever he was talking about.

He explained that since I was into channelling and spiritual writing, there would be a certain sense of perception and expectation of how I should behave, speak and conduct myself.

So I told him that I make it a point to mention and write that I smoke, drink, swear and am basically inherently flawed.

I remember he smiled, clapped and said, 'Boss, you are a wise man, much wiser that your age and how you look.'

Then he told me his experience. When the Ramayana series became famous, when nobody left their homes but sat in front of their television sets, watching the lives of Shri Ram, Sita Maa and Lord Hanuman unfold, the world suddenly began to perceive him, Ramanand Sagar, in a different light. Whenever he was invited for an event, he would be served pure vegetarian food with a glass of juice. Now, he was a normal man with a good appetite for meat and alcohol. For a long time, he allowed the perceptions of others to lead his life.

'Then one day, I got fed up. I love my food and drink. But people fed me the so-called sattvic food. One day, while I was staying with a family in London, I was asked what I would like to eat. I told myself, "To hell with what others think. I am going to begin living my life." I then told them, "Get me my scotch and then a good meal of grilled chicken." I thought they would pass out but in a short while things began to get normal. So remember, boss, do not try to live up to the expectations of the world that surrounds you.'

For anybody who is following the path of spirituality, one needs to be most careful about getting entangled in this dual web created by others for their self-centred reasons. I believe that unless you are a Perfect Master, you are going to be inherently flawed, with numerous weaknesses and limitations. But people around you and me are going to make us believe that we are God, Godsend and beyond flaws. If you fall into this entrapment, either out of ego or stupidity, you are doomed, as there is no way you are going to match up to the hue of divinity and Godhood these chaps have enforced upon you. It is best to be your normal self, even if you often behave like an exceedingly temperamental ass. Do not try to live up to or meet their views of yourself, as those views are not about you. They are what they want to believe to meet their expectations and sense of insecurities. They are going to put you up on the pedestal, and if you do a little wrong, they are going to first piss on the pedestal, then pour gasoline and burn you to a beautiful grilled mass of meat. I mean they have not even spared God. Who the hell are you and me to survive this onslaught of unfair perceptions and expectations?

I remember once somebody told me, 'You pray so much but you still curse like a street urchin.' All I could tell the individual was, 'If after praying so much, I can be so foul-mouthed, imagine how much more abusive I would have been if I did not pray.'

Perceptions and expectations are a pit of quicksand which the most popular as well as the most humble individuals have to consciously grapple.

If we fall into their trap, we will never live our lives, but the lives others want us to live to be loved, liked and accepted by others. I guess that is the worst way to live. To live trying to win a brownie point, or not hurt somebody's opinion and belief of who we are, or worse, to begin to believe their perceptions about us is the surest way to hell and ulcers. It is like a slow virus that consumes our soul and our very inherent, independent being.

The world will use guilt and tears to tear you down and make you walk their path of perceptions and expectations. Do not get sucked into all this. Try to live your life. Yes, try not to hurt others. Try to be a good human being. But most important of all, do not try to fool yourself. That is the worst path to take because you are then deceiving yourself; your every thought, word and action will come from deceit as you have made a world based on the world's perception or worse, your own false perception of who you are.

Perception and expectations of the world and your own illusions about yourself and your inherent strengths, weakness and limitations, put together, is In short creating a monster of darkness and gloom.

Thus, avoid living in anybody's perceptions and expectations, including you. First and foremost, know who you truly are: your strengths, weaknesses and limitations. Once you are aware of yourself, walk your path. You might fall, you might fail, but you will be walking your path, aware that you are responsible for your injuries. You are dancing to your own rhythm and you will be exceedingly aware of who is trying to manipulate you consciously or unconsciously.

I know it is hard. I grapple with this each day. But being aware that we have to live our lives and make the most of it will slowly free us from the clutches of the views and opinions of the world around us, and slowly, the leash around our necks will loosen and one day we will be truly free.

Till then bow wow.

Be blessed.

The simple philosophy for a sane life is to not let somebody else's perceptions of you become your reality; no matter how hard you try, you are never going to live up to the expectations of others.

Perception and expectations of the world and your own illusions about yourself and your inherent strengths, weakness and limitations, put together, is in short creating a monster of darkness and gloom.

To live trying to win a brownie point, or not hurt somebody's opinion and belief of who we are, or worse, to begin to believe their perceptions about us is the surest way to hell and ulcers. It is like a slow virus that consumes our soul and our very inherent, independent being.

9

The Ether Element

I met Bapuji, the reclusive sage from Ahmedabad one day and our collaboration bore fruit in the form of a book named, *The Aum Of All Things*. Bapuji was a part of the income tax department till he left everything and began his pursuit of Oneness. We were in his room. I sat on the bed with him, while the others sat on chairs around us. He made sure that I had a blanket wrapped around me and a skull cap on my head, as it was freezing cold in Delhi. I was keen to know about the five elements or the '*Panch Tatvas*' in our environment and within us.

'So in the Tatvas, first came Divine Ether or Divine Space (or the element of Divine Silence, as Baba Sai of Shirdi calls it) and then came the element of Divine Air. From the element of Divine Air, the element of Divine Fire or *Agni* Tatva was created.'

One must understand that when an individual soul moves forth from the Divine Source, it is first filled or made up of only one element—the element of divinity or Prime Ether. This element, which is also called the element of space, is one of the least understood elements in the five-elemental theory in this phase of the cycle of time. One can quantify Air, Fire, Water and Earth, but how does one quantify space?

According to Baba Sai of Shirdi, space or the element of Ether is basically the element of divinity in a form (though space does not have a form, it fills two forms within itself). Thus, the invisible element of space or Ether is the first element that was created by the Boss Man and hence is the closest to representing His/Her form and individuality, which an individual—either body or soul—can ever reach. Thus, each religion, each spiritual Guru and each ancient text keep insisting every individual to go within and strengthen the element of Ether by being silent. I guess that instead of telling one and all through the scriptures to 'shut the fug up', the polite terminology is to call it the element of Ether.

So first came the Divine Ether, and through that the rest followed. Basically, this also follows the philosophy that whatever is present in the subtle world eventually manifests itself in the physical gross world. But first, it starts with the Divine Elements which manifest Themselves as Subtle Elements, which in turn manifest as Gross Elements. For instance, first comes the thought, which gives rise to intent or feelings or desires, which gets converted into effort, which turns into one's attitude, which comes out through action, which then leads to a pattern of habit and eventually that becomes one's personality. Of course, most of us feel that we do not think first, but in reality, we are so habituated to a pattern of thinking that we do not realize that we have created a thought in a fraction of a second. Thus what manifests comes forth from impulsive reactions, and we go through life like yaks high on hemp.

'Thus from Divine Ether came forth Divine Air, from which came forth Divine Fire. The Air Element encompasses the Fire Element as well. Helium is created from hydrogen, am I right? H_2 is converted to H_3, right?'

Yeah, right. That is why I am writing blogs on spirituality.

This is the reason why a candle kept in a closed glass bottle or box dies out in a few seconds. Fire needs the element of Air to burn.

'So without the element of Air, you cannot have the element of Fire?' I wanted to move away from the topic of helium as quickly as possible. 'We have Fire inside *Vayu* (Air) when it generates electricity? So what you are trying to tell me is that if there is no Air, then there will be no Fire?'

'Yes. That is why the Vayu Tatva has been created before Agni (Fire). Initially, how were the elements created? They were created because of *sankalps* (intentions and desires) which had begun to germinate. With sankalps came Param *Akash* or Divine Ether, from which came Param Vayu or Divine Wind or Air, from which came Param Agni or Divine Fire (for the record, now we only have Ether, Air and Fire as part of the five-elemental world; Divine or Param is no longer present in the elements). For instance, we all have heard of ancient musicians who, through certain *Ragas* (ancient Indian musical compositions), would bring down rain or light oil lamps. When the Deepak Raga was played or sung, the power which the music generated would light lamps, while the rendering of Malhar Raga would bring rain. So inside the element of Air, the element of Water is also present. H_2O is the formula, right? It is the merging of hydrogen and oxygen—the constitution of the elements of water. H_2O is made from Vayu.'

'It is obvious that there is water in the Air Element. But is there Fire too in the Air Element?' I inquired. Anything to get away from hydrogen and oxygen.

'Yes. So, Water and Fire are both present in the Air Element, which in turn is present in the element of Ether or space.

Mother Earth is the combination of all elements. Gradually, as all elements came into being, the atmas began to multiply,' said Bapuji.

What Bapuji wanted to convey was that as souls began to multiply, individual desires began to take control over the soul and as individual desires grew, the divine power started to dwindle. From desires came the need to possess, and through the desire to possess, everything went wrong.

'Our scriptures say that there are *Anant Koti Brahmands* in existence. Which means there are countless or trillions of galaxies in Creation and that trillions of Creations are made and destroyed from time to time. If there are trillions of galaxies according to the scriptures, then logically that means there are Anant Koti Shivas or countless Demi Creators too. So there are Shivas or Creators and then there is Maha Maha Maha Shiva or the Absolute Authority. That's why we celebrate Mahashivratri once a year, even though Shivratri comes every month.

'Shiva or the Creator made the world of the five Gross Elements. He takes the whole Creation into Himself, just as the Black Hole engulfs millions of Creations. Why are we unhappy? The main reason is that the five elements that make our bodies have got polluted and filled with negativity. The air we breathe and the water we drink are polluted. This is bound to affect our emotional, mental and physical state,' said Bapuji.

The logic is simple. As we are made out of the five elements, to operate at a level of optimum capacity, the raw material and fuel that keeps each of the five elements in prime health have to be top-class. We may have the most powerful and fancy sports car, but if the fuel being pumped into the car is suspect and adulterated, the car's performance is initially going to be slightly below par. Gradually, the capacity is going to drop till a day comes when the poor metallic bastard stalls forever.

Our physical five-elemental body thrives on the five elements in our world, which in turn thrives on the elements in the subtle world; if the root supply is contaminated, we as human beings will move further and further away from our real source and identity.

That is why it is said that while cooking food, one should constantly chant the name or be in a state of prayer, and be one with The One. This helps to bring down the divinity through the food which is made up of the five elements. The mind can be elsewhere, preoccupied with different thoughts, while we go through the process of cooking. Hence, one needs to take care of the energy, thoughts and feelings while cooking to ensure the purity of the elements going in the body. Some call it sattvic food. It isn't about what one cooks or eats, it's about the energy using which one cooks it, which is then consumed by the body through the elements.

We cannot change the five elements in the cosmos. What we can do is strengthen the one element, which fortunately is the most pivotal element—the element of Ether, space, void, silence . . . the element of divinity.

As we move deeper into the Oasis of Silence, the element of divinity within us begins to get fortified and nourished, which in turn infuses it in the other four elements, strengthening them. This allows us to tap into the subtle elements that exist in the spirit world, which then allows us to tap into the Prime Elements, which in turn allows us to tap into the divine and prime element of Ether or space. This which is where we have first come forth from—the Big Trumpeter, who for some reason 'bajaoed all our bands' (put us in a situation) by trying to get creative and was under the illusion that mankind will be able to handle the concept of Creation and free will, thereby converting an oasis into a cesspit of depravity.

Now when I keep harping about silence, I do not mean you have to become dumb or let everybody walk over you. I don't mean that you should not speak your mind or not stand up for your dignity. Being silent means being silent within—where you are in the moment and where your mind is not an expressway of thoughts, clanging, clashing and circumventing each other all the time. An individual may be constantly communicating with the world, but may be as silent as a tomb within, constantly in the moment or chanting the God, Goddess or Master's name. When you are in the state of constant silence within, calmly accepting all, knowing that all is transitory, the element of Ether or divinity slowly begins to grow, strengthening the other elements or tapping into the source of the subtle element of Ether, which further gets strengthened by the Divine Ether.

Once you are in tune with Divine Silence, all knowledge, power, radiance, goodness and the very essence of Oneness begin to fill the individual; it is through Divine Silence that the Masters know the past, present and the future.

'This happens once and only comes through The One. The divinity of the Ultimate Father and Mother comes through the way He/She imparts knowledge. Now how do you know that the Creator is the ultimate authority and the right one? Through the awakening of the Third-Eye Chakra, which is gained through meditation, He/She gives us the knowledge of the New World. We have come from Amar Lok or from immortality to Mrutyu Lok, the land of death. How was the world created? Where are the deities? How was our soul created? One can get all these answers via *dhyan* or meditation,' said Bapuji.

'When Lord Krishna came down to Earth, what did He say? He said, "This war between truth and untruth, I cannot stop. This Mahabharata war, I cannot stop." Now today, the *Devatas* or Demi Gods have descended upon Earth. Imagine if

Lord Krishna could not stop the Mahabharata war, then who is going to be able to stop this degeneration that one sees within and all around?'

I believe that the one who goes deep within, meditates, becomes one with his/her breath, merges with his/her breath, thus becoming one with the Source and through the Source, taps into the universal grid of knowledge, can go beyond man and become superman or Godlike, as we would say in earlier days. The Mahabharata really is within one's self. The five brothers or Pandavas stand for the five senses. The day you bring your five senses under your control and give this power neither to an external force, person, thing nor object, then the innumerable emotions and desires—one can call them Kauravas—cease to have a hold on you and you are free to soar. True freedom is when one's state of mind does not get affected or influenced by happiness or sadness. The problem is that this is so simple to achieve that most of us are never going to achieve it as we have lost all respect for simplicity and are into designer stuff—be it designer meditation, healing, cults, religions. The old-fashioned simple stuff does not appeal to us any more. So yoga has to become power yoga and steam yoga, meditation has various fancy names added to it, and pranic healing has to become some fancy Italian form of healing. The simple stuff of sitting in a corner, going within and becoming one with the breath is not in vogue any more. You can dress a horse in a Ralph Lauren limited spring collection edition, but the fact remains that it is still going to be a horse and is never going to clean up after crapping all over the place. Look around: most people have become spiritual shoppers when the answer truly just lies in going within. Focusing on the breath or one's Master, and becoming one with the breath and Master is the only way out. Ok, enough of my ramblings.

'Now what will happen? What do we have? We have our soul, which comprises the mind, intellect and *sanskar,* and expresses itself through the different bodies which are made up of different combinations of the elements. We need to connect with The One, with Divine Vision and Divine Knowledge, to go about this transformation from a state of death to a deathless or immortal state. We want to bring the Param Tatvas or Divine Elements, Divine Radiance and Light into the world. The transformation has to come about through the purity in the elements. The only way is to meditate, visualize and become one with the Absolute Authority. Then through the power of affirmations and visualizations, one can bring down the Prime Elements and spread it through all of Creation.'

We have come from the Divine Prime Elements, starting from Divine Ether or Divine Silence. When we go silent within, we begin to raise the Ether Element within us, which first allows the other four Elements to be in harmony with each other. The Ether Element or God Element, as Baba calls it, slowly allows one to tap into the Divine Elements, infusing the individual with various powers and superhuman capabilities; the individual begins to connect with the Prime Elements through the element of silence. The more silent you become within, you once again start moving closer and closer towards the Absolute One—first you slowly start consolidating yourself into Divine Ether as our first element of individuality was Divine Ether or Divine Silence. When you bring forth Divine Silence within, we start moving towards our Source and eventually become one with the Source.

Be blessed always.

When an individual soul moves forth from the Divine Source, it is first filled with or made up of only one element—the element of divinity or Prime Ether.

When you are in the state of constant silence within, calmly accepting all, knowing that all is transitory, the element of Ether or divinity slowly begins to grow.

Our first element of individuality was only Divine Ether or Divine Silence. When you bring forth Divine Silence within, we start moving towards our Source and eventually become one with the Source.

<h1 style="text-align:center">10</h1>

The Three Bodies That Encase the Soul

So back to Bapuji and our conversation about the elements and how the various elements affect not only our physical body but also our astral (emotional vehicle) and causal (mental and karmic) body.

'Our body has a subtle (astral) body and a causal body. There are seven different types of cosmic powers residing in the causal body. The cosmic energies that are there in the atmosphere automatically charge each one's causal body. The causal body runs the three-elemental subtle (astral) body and the subtle body runs the five-elemental gross body. The origin of all physical ailments or diseases is in the causal body and then through the astral body affects the physical body.

'The causal body is made of Param Akash (Prime Ether), Param Vayu (Prime Wind or Air) and Param Agni (Prime Fire) elements. When the Param Akash Tatva gets corrupted due to tension, stress, jealousy, lust, anger and hunger for various things, including too much of talking and gossiping, we suffer from all types of serious diseases. The deficit of the Param Akash Tatva causes most of the diseases.

'First, the disease attacks or gets ingrained into the causal body. That is because it's the first layering of one's body and also the most subtle. Closest to the soul is the Param Akash Tatva, then Param Vayu Tatva and then the Param Agni Tatva. When the individual increases his/her wants and desires, he/she gets agitated. He/she screams, shouts and becomes restless, leading to an imbalance in the Param Akash Tatva, which is responsible for peace and calmness within one's self.

'So that's why the sages would close their eyes and be in their *Divya Swarup* or Divine State. There is a chain reaction when the Prime Ether Element is affected—it affects the Prime Wind and Prime Fire Element as well. That is why the causal body is called "causal" for it is caused by and reacts to our sankalps or desires or intentions. What is the solution for this corruption within the causal body, *beta*?

'Go within. Meditate. Be calm. Be peaceful, joyous and positive. Surrender to whatever the Master has in store for you, while still giving life your 100 per cent,' I replied. Or just get sloshed and high, I mused.

'All the experiences and conditioning of your previous births or sanskars are in the causal body. It is in the 75,000-crore cells contained in the causal body. Tell me, what are these cells made up of?'

Knowing me, most of the crore cells in the causal body must be made of nicotine, good herbs and various potable spirits. I kept quiet. I smiled as though I knew what Bapuji was talking about. The best way to go about this was to look with deep intent eyes, nod and then gently caress your temple.

'The cells are made up of Prime Elements or Param Tatvas. Thus this Param Tatva body is the causal body that covers your soul. Now, when the quantity of Prime Fire Element or Param Agni Tatva increases in the physical or astral body, it brings negativity in the subtle and physical bodies and one tends to experience anger, negativity, depression, etc. *Vairagya Vruti* or disenchantment comes when one is silent within and outside, as one fills oneself up with more Akash Tatva. Agni Tatva and Vayu Tatva are responsible to convert disenchantment into maya or illusion and thus get the body entangled more in bodily relations.'

Basically, what Bapuji meant was that when desires and attachment increase, the heat of all these emotions, wants, expectations and frustrations brings about an increase in the Fire Element within the body. This leads to an increase in the Wind Element. Both Fire and Wind Elements distance us from The One and brings us closer to the world and all that which the world has to offer or entice. It is only the Ether Element that takes us closer to The One. The sages say that all our karma is stored in the causal body. If you want to work on your karma without going by the laws of cause and effect, then the only way out is to work on your causal body. How does one do that?

Baba Sai says in channelling that through the power of silence, calmness, chanting and meditation, a Divine Fire (not to be confused with the Fire Element) burns away the karma that is encased in the causal body. Both good and bad karma are burnt away, making your slate as pristine as it was when the spark left the Great Flame.

So all illnesses are stored in the causal body. When your causal body is cleansed, all illnesses related to mental, emotional and physical bodies are removed too. But first the causal body needs to be repaired and cleansed. If that takes place, then the illness is booted out of the system forever. How does one go about strengthening one's causal body? We go back to silence.

'Thus one can make changes within one's self to increase the Akash Tatva and by consciously remaining calm, silent and content, one can bring about subtle changes in the astral and causal levels too. One can, through one's sankalps and intentions, recall one's Divine State and meditate on one's seed body—the Divine Body—by making one a satellite of the Absolute Authority. Once the amount of Param Tatvas reaches its maximum level, then the energy will gradually transcend, and your causal and subtle body will get charged. If the soul is charged, it means that all the three Param Tatvas within oneself have got balanced. Once the Param Tatvas are balanced, the physical body will automatically become light and get charged.

'Regular meditation will give temporary relief to our five-elemental body, but if we study the main cause of the diseases, we realize that one needs to first focus on repairing the causal body. Once that is done, all the diseases from the astral and physical body can be removed too. In fact, the astral and gross body will automatically heal once the causal body is filled completely with the Param Tatvas. This can happen only when one truly works on the causal body first. Impurity is the cause of all illnesses and ailments. The main reason for man's downfall is that he is entangled in the body and bodily relations. So first and foremost, one needs to get detached from them.'

Ok, I need to add something here. I feel the root cause of all issues is not attachment with the outside world, but attachment to your own self. In reality, we love ourselves the most. One needs to get detached from one's own ego, thoughts, wants, wishes and feelings. One needs to understand that when one feels something is right from their point of view and for the loved one's benefit, they need to understand that it is from their point of view. Attachment is also wanting someone to do what they want under the term of 'love and care', overlooking the loved one's strengths, weaknesses, sanskar, past experiences and will power—most importantly, forgetting what the loved one feels about it.

Once you get detached from your own self, worldly attachments will automatically drop from all the bodies. You love your child because he/she is your child. If something happens to him/her, you feel restless and disoriented, and that makes you yearn for the good health of all your loved ones. In reality, your sanity and state of centredness depend on the well-being of your loved ones.

Let's take this example of a friend of mine who was head over heels in love with his dog. Whenever we met, he would keep praising the dog and shower endearments on the animal. If the dog was ill, this friend would be depressed and worried. Then it so happened that for over a month or so, there was no conversation about the dog. Sometime later I got to know from his brother that the dog was put to sleep. I was surprised as I used to meet my friend regularly and there was no mention of the demise of his favourite dog, who he often proclaimed to love more than his life. The brother filled me up with what had happened. The dog suffered from some illness in the brain. For some reason which I can't fathom, whenever the dog saw my friend, it would bark loudly and rush to bite him. It once even charged and badly scratched my friend. This became a routine and it reached a point where they had to tie the dog whenever my friend was home. Even then the dog would growl and bark at him. The poor dog wasn't well. It was disoriented and later on my friend insisted that the dog be put down.

When I spoke to him about it, he began to abuse the dog and said that he didn't want to talk about it. Where did all the love and attachment for the dog disappear in a span of two months? The fact is that the friend loved the dog's love and attachment towards himself. When that love and attachment turned into growls, bites and visible hate, the love went out of the window. We love ourselves and through our love for ourselves, we identify who we love and who we don't. Of course there are exceptions, but from what I have seen of life, this is sort of a rule.

Back to Bapuji.

'Become the image of the soul. The soul is encased in the causal body. Remember the Paramatma—you will think what you see and what you think you will become. Think of your Divine Self even while you eat or sleep, and believe that you are living in the Divine Land. You will gain Divine Intellect and the causal body will get power. Golden cosmic light means golden Param Tatva. The quantity of Akash Tatva is more in the golden cosmic zone. Param Vayu Tatva is dark blue and Param Agni is red in colour; there are seven such bodies inside the causal body. The cosmic powers will come to you by just thinking of the Creator's formless state. It is important to take a sankalp where one imagines one's causal and astral body first being charged and then gaining power from the Creator.

'If the individual thinks and creates good thoughts, then the atmosphere's golden cosmic energy enters the individual's causal body. If the soul thinks creative and positive thoughts, then multi-coloured cosmic energy enters the causal body. If the soul is calm, then green cosmic rays enter the causal body and if anger prevails, then the atmosphere's red cosmic rays enter the causal body. Nowadays, there are souls that enter another body and make the unsuspecting individual perform actions, either through anger or lust, which the individual would repent later on. He/she would keep wondering how they could have done this thing! In reality, he/she hasn't done anything. Another spirit had occupied the individual's body and performed the gory act. It also means that another spirit used the platform of an individual's mind which was encased with anger to do what it wanted to do. That is why being calm and centred is so important at every moment.

Likewise, there are noble souls who enter physical bodies to get good work performed. These souls use the human body as a medium or vehicle to either do good things or to spread the Light. They need a calm mind to operate through.

'If a pregnant mother thinks negatively or is filled with negative thoughts, then black cosmic rays enter the child's body from the atmosphere; the mother transfers black cosmic energy through her ears to the child. Sometimes when a person is born, the causal body of the individual, through past-life karma, may have many negative traits and thoughts. We call this 'inborn nature', which is actually past-life patterns and karma showcasing in this lifetime. If it is a great soul, then the individual will come with greatness and noble traits in his/her causal and astral aura, which will automatically make him/her perform noble deeds.

'Creation takes place via the causal cells. The related physical part of the body gets infected, as the level of Param Tatvas in the causal body have got affected. This leads to paralysis, cancer and various other diseases. Let us assume that the brain area of the causal body has got affected. Automatically, the brain area of the subtle or astral body gets affected, leading to brain tumour, Parkinson's, Alzheimer's, dementia, memory loss, etc.

'How can one cure illnesses of the gross body? Through the Mun. Mun means the heart. The soul has the knowledge that it has to focus on its subtle and causal body, and its Divine Self to gain or regain power. But it cannot remember its own divinity. Why is it so? It has the desire. It has the knowledge. But why is it unable to remember its divinity?

'Take the example of a normal human being. Why is the soul unable to think of its subtle and Divine Self? It is because its intellect, mind and consciousness keeps getting attracted or attached to the demands of the body, family, friends, detractors, enemies, new cars or contracts and so on and so forth. The negative load caused by the karmic baggage of past lives or wrong use of one's free will or the agony of those whose loved ones are calling out to them, individually or collectively, weighs down the causal body and it gets filled with black cosmic energy. Even though one may not wish for this, our mind gets diverted to the body and bodily relations due to this energy.

'So who makes one unhappy? We know the reason and the solution of our unhappiness. In reality, we have the knowledge of both. But one cannot start performing *yog* only with knowledge. Why? Because we repeatedly keep falling into the trap of maya.

'Who or what is maya?' Bapuji asked to nobody in particular.

Ok, back to my two-bit talk. According to me, maya or illusion is anything that distracts you from your only worthwhile objective in life—merging with and serving the Master and the Creator. But my take on this very controversial woman called maya is this: as long as you are never distracted from merging with and serving your Master and Creator, you can go about having a blast in life and still be a yogi. My logic is simple. Whether you are in prayer or in a cafe, be true to yourself; be aware that your Master is with you, and be in the moment and enjoy it.

If maya revolves around the five elements, then we are doomed if we are eating food or drinking a good absinthe or malt. So what if you are having a drink? He/she doesn't become any less spiritual than someone having boiled water. The important thing is to never forget your objective to make your Master happy and proud of you. Be good and have a blast. Trust me, the God and the Master enjoy a good time. God is not some rigid accountant. Our sages would have a rollicking time with *Somras* and hash. They never let go of their main priority and that is to make the Master happy and proud of them, and to merge with the Old Rock Star.

Now if you follow my walk, one of the two things will happen. We will either reach our Master with a smile plastered on our face or we will get our astral asses busted, once again with a smile on our face, with a band of folks who enjoy a good life. Don't get confused with spirituality and ritual, tradition and superstition. Convert maya into a friend. Have a good time and still merge. Don't become all serious and adultlike. Adulthood is the root cause of indigestion, superstition, violence and boredom. Be a kid at heart. Be pure, but have a blast. Yes, I agree that through meditation, visualization and affirmation, a lot of good can be done for oneself and all of Creation. Spread right thoughts, whether you are in the physical body or you have visualized yourself with and in the Creator. Pray for peace as we really need it. People are dying in the name of God. Kids are dying because there is no clean drinking water or food. Children are being forced to beg after being put through torture. Most of the politicians do not care for human life or human dignity. We cannot do much to make good the wrong in the physical world, but we have the power in the spirit world to do good. Through prayers, meditation and affirmations, yes, in our own humble way, we can all do a lot of good for Mother Earth who has been pillaged, mutilated and violated, along with most of her children who are voiceless and have no say in the larger scheme of things. Pray and wish for good and don't stop at Mother Earth, but include all of Creation. I firmly believe that when a child smiles, a star some place in Creation becomes slightly brighter.

Be blessed.

> *The very word 'causal' comes from cause and effect. So, all our karmas are stored in the causal body. If you want to work on your karma without going by the laws of cause and effect, then the only way out is to work on your causal body.*
>
> *The root cause of all issues is not attachment with the outside world, but attachment to your own self. In reality, we love ourselves the most. One needs to get detached from one's own ego, thoughts, wants, wishes, feelings.*
>
> *All illnesses are stored in the causal body. When your causal body is cleansed, all illnesses related to mental, emotional and physical bodies are removed too.*

11

Giving Satan an Inferiority Complex

I have realized through my mistakes, blunders, impulsive temperament, weaknesses and limitations that I am instrumental in causing anguish to myself and building the foundations of discord within me. I believe this may be true for you too. Forget the laws of cause and effect and the ramifications of free will; most often, our own imbecility creates our personal grief and makes us see glimpses of hell within our very being. We don't need to truly die to experience hell as we have mastered the art of creating hell for ourselves and those around us.

We are so blind to the simple truths of life that we keep spending lifetimes in the petty and self-destructive by-lanes, leaving the highway of centredness and true joy far behind.

A dear boy who came for channelling asked me when he would find a Guru, the same way Paramhansa Yogananda met His Guru Sri Yukteswar Giri. The answer that came forth was simple. First and foremost, one needs to have lived a life with such profound use of free will that one's karmic balance sheet permits the presence of such a Guru. Secondly, the intensity and yearning for a true Master should be so overpowering that

73

it forces the Old Chap to enter your life. And most importantly, the Guru knows when the disciple is ready to embrace His/Her presence in his/her life. This has got nothing to do with the love a Guru feels for His/Her disciple. Love remains constant for all. Only the disciple's state of acceptance and being in the state of nothingness decides to what intensity the Master projects His/Her presence.

The boy agreed and then said he wanted a Guru to teach him how to live a spiritual life. The answer to this was simple too. The Guru will first make you unlearn all that is ingrained in you. He will not make you learn anything as all that you need to learn has already been programmed into your spiritual DNA. What the Guru will do is make you unlearn lifetimes of conditioning—a poisonous amalgamation of desires and yearnings that take you away from the simple truths of life. The Master knows that till the child lets go of creating his/her own personal hell, the glimpse of heaven is light years away.

What we see is not necessarily true. We all know that the sun never rises or sets, but we see the sun rising and setting, or what appears to be the sun rising and setting. In reality, it is the earth moving. As in *The Fakir*, Baba tells Rudra: darkness comes about not because the sun has set but because that part of the earth has shown its back to the sun. Similarly, the eternal truth is that sadness, pain, anguish, and ill health of body and mind come about not because our God, Goddess or Master has left us, but because we have moved away from the eternal source of Light.

We all know this truth, but we are so comfortable with our heads in our arses that God and the heavens can very well wait.

I mean, we all know we can carry only our karma with us when we have life kicked out of us, but most of us give least importance to the use of our free will and karma, and strive for everything else in the bargain. Imagine if a friend had to traverse through a desert on a very temperamental and hypersensitive camel. You would advise your friend to carry maximum quantum of water, apart from a really effective sunscreen and a stun gun for the camel. Not to forget food and the right clothes. Now what if the friend just took a bottle of water and carried a large quantity of everything else? What would you think of the IQ level of that friend? Guess what, we are all that friend. We screw up big time in the only journey that matters.

Each one of us knows the eternal truth, but we still go about life, moving away from all that which is good and right for one's true well-being. We then bemoan our destiny and the lack of love and grace of The One.

When a Guru enters your life, He/She strives to declutter your very being of all that which takes you away from the simple foundation of all that which is spiritual. There are three principles that Prophet Zarathustra, known as the first Prophet, told His followers nearly three thousand years before the birth of Lord Christ.

The three simple foundations for all spirituality are good thoughts, good words and good deeds.

I believe He wanted to tell all of Creation that no matter what, if you operated through good thoughts, words and deeds, you were truly sorted in this life and the next, be it in the physical plane or in any of the seven dimensions.

I believe all scriptures have been trying to say the same thing—if we can try to adhere to this simple principle of living, it would put a smile on God's face or make His Radiance glow a little bit brighter.

Good thoughts, words and deeds basically mean that you have to try to come from a place of well-being for one and all—in your mind, speech and action. But when can one come from a state of well-being for one and all? It is when one does not discriminate, judge or slander another person and comes from a place of compassion, love and understanding.

It is a simple philosophy that Lord Christ spoke of more than two thousand years ago when He said, 'Do unto others what you would want others to do to you and your loved ones.'

It is a simple philosophy and if followed, one's life would truly brim with good thoughts, words and deeds. As we all would like to be thought well of by one's loved ones and the world at large, we would all like to be spoken well of with love, politeness and tenderness, and we would all love to treated well, with compassion and with a large heart. I mean, how much more simple can this get?

Simple stuff but we have gone and screwed it up nice and good.

We are so filled with pettiness that the devil stands dumbfounded and jobless. We are doing his job so proficiently that he has begun to get an inferiority complex. Why would he not?

Imagine how the devil must feel when more people have been killed in the name of God than in his own name? Go through history and It is clear that millions have been massacred in God's name. Monsieur Satan can go boil his head along with his horns as he can claim no such thing.

Imagine what a loser Satan must feel like when only a few want to kill in his name and most of them need to be on psychiatric medication to do so. But look at the armies of devotees who go completely blood thirsty the moment God's name is mentioned, choosing the most ingenious ways to kill, maim, rape, bomb and murder . . . all in God's name.

And his own empire, Hell Private Limited, is empty, as we have created our own personal hell, innumerable times more ghastly and gory than what he could ever have thought of.

By making our lives complicated with our personal egos, petty thoughts, slander, hate, envy, lust and greed, we truly have left the devil feeling incapacitated, dismembered and thus rather impotent.

I don't know if any of this makes sense to you, but it has been a long time since anything made sense to me for sure. I mean, why are we so incapable of the philosophy, 'live and let live'? We can't stop judging and resorting to slander, and still we believe we are decent God-loving folks?

Why are we incapable of spreading happiness and joy for the sake of spreading happiness and joy and not to meet one's own personal agenda?

Why has life become so complicated that one needs to go to a very expensive resort to get one's breath back?

What is the matter with us that we have made the devil feel incapacitated and cheated out of his own throne and empire? The best part of it all is that we do so in the name of love, honour, self-respect, family and yes, in the name of God.

The futility of existence has never been experienced by so many in history as it is felt now. Thus, it is little wonder that for many, life, love and fate are merely four-letter words.

If God was aware that this age of darkness, called *Kalyug*, would dawn, and mankind would behave in the manner we are behaving, why did the Creator go about His/Her job of Creation?

The only logical answer I can accept and find an iota of rationale in is that God wanted to show Satan that there is nothing Satan can do which God can't do better.

The books say mankind is God's greatest Creation. I guess I have to agree because if the devil was under the illusion that he was the king of hell and creator of all suffering, then he obviously needed to be shown reality; creation of mankind has been the final nail in the coffin of the devil, as the two-horned bastard has been made redundant by the ingenious mankind.

> *We are so blind to the simple truths of life that we keep spending lifetimes in the petty and self-destructive by-lanes, leaving the highway of centredness and true joy far behind.*
>
> *The eternal truth is that sadness, pain, anguish, and ill health of body and mind come about not because our God, Goddess or Master have left us, but because we have moved away from the eternal source of Light.*
>
> *The three simple foundations for all spirituality are good thoughts, good words and good deeds.*

12

Growing Old Is Optional

When I am truly down and out. When the futility of existence becomes overpowering. When the day seems to be an eternity of misty by-lanes that lead nowhere. When I begin to question the permanence of the heavens above and the foolhardiness of Creation. When I question my intent of all that which I have thought, spoken and done, and begin to realize that more than often it has been vanity, false pride and manipulative self-centredness that has been the fountain from which all this has sprung forth. When being an adult seems nothing but a deceitful admonition and all I want to do is shut my eyes and be obliterated, not just from the body but even from the spirit. Not merge. Not attain Nirvana. Not have the gorgeous Kundalini dance about from the Root to the Crown Chakra and back. All I want is to be permanently erased from the DNA of existence . . . never was, is or will be in a state of consciousness . . .

. . . That is the time I realize how badly I have screwed up the fundamentals of inherent spirituality and Godhood . . . by forgetting to hold on, cling on, hang on to the madness, the joy and the eternal spring of being a child.

If there is anything that has corrupted our spirituality, our sanity, our purity, our humaneness, our everything, it is by allowing life, family, friends, colleagues, strangers, the media, politicians and the manipulators of spirituality and religion to take away our childlike state of being and thrust upon us the callous version of existence called adulthood.

By no means am I trying to generalize that all kids are children at heart. Most of the kids I know now scare me with their lack of innocence. Even in such cases, it is the absence of joy, innocence, compassion and madness in the child that makes the child behave like an adult—mean, empty and slanderous.

The first thing to go when the claws of adulthood get hold of us is the joyous and orgasmic ability to laugh aloud for the most inane reasons. There has to be a good reason to laugh and as we get mauled by fate, life, spouse, kids, income tax, alimony, employers, lovers and the so-called safe keepers of morality and religion, we lose the ability to laugh till tears roll down our cheeks. We forget what it is to howl out loud by thumping the ground with our feet or slapping the table or the backs of those around for no reason. But something triggered the funny bone and laughter gushed out of us, like trapped fizz from a champagne bottle.

My entire childhood was filled with laughter and oh boy, how we laughed. Even now for me, a good day is when I am with my daughter or with my bunch of friends . . . ageing hippies . . . and we have a good laugh at something the adults will not approve of or even get . . . that is a day well spent.

I am so tired of everybody taking everything so seriously that I truly want to begin consuming ridiculous quantum of absinthe or smoke up some nice stuff from Manali and be in that state of carefree childlike joy, far away from: 'Oh I am so sane, spiritual and mature'. Yes, yes, yes, I know that this is not the right attitude or guidance, but you know what I mean.

Every time one opens his/her mouth, there is someone waiting with a comment or an opinion. Slander is the norm of the day. And the best part is that we will do it in the name of God or love or purity or anything . . . it truly doesn't matter . . . we can't keep our inherent rotting garbage to ourselves.

When did the joy and laughter dry out of me or out of you? When did putting somebody down become equivalent to uplifting yourself? When did hundred lies truly become the truth?

The other day, I told my daughter Meher what I have been telling her since she could understand my nonsense—baby, art in any form is more interesting than most human beings. So be very careful when you associate yourself with human beings as they can infect you with their adulthood and there is nothing that sucks the essence and fragrance out of life as growing old in the spirit.

Sai Baba of Shirdi told a friend once through channelling that there are three things to avoid if one wants to become a better human, a higher spiritual being or an Angel, and there are three things one must indulge in if one wants to truly enjoy physical, emotional, mental and spiritual life.

The first thing mentioned to truly engage with the vitality of life, be it in the body or in the spirit dimensions, is to be able to find joy in the basics. To be able to see the humour in everything, as life, fate and the Master have a strange sense of humour.

When the Bible says that you need to be a child to find a place in heaven, I believe what Lord Christ meant was that one had to be childlike and not be a boring adult to find a place in the highest spiritual dimension. That one had to be filled with childlike wonder, joy and gratitude, and not be contaminated with the virus of manipulation, greed and play the victim role that adults do so well. To be a child means never growing old in spirit. It has nothing to do with age of the body or matter. It means never letting the aura of wonderment and cheerfulness leave you even if life, fate or morons are kicking the holy crap out of you.

I know life can be harsh and often all one hopes is to never wake up. But if one has to live, then one has to forge ahead with one's head held high, a smile in one's eyes and joy in the heart. If a movie, a book or a cup of chai with a friend or even oneself can bring about joy, when prayers and meditation cannot, so be it. Remember the spirit within needs to be nurtured and no amount of worldly glory or power or wealth or indulging in slander is going to make one radiate joy.

The fact that the babble and prattle of a child has brought about more smiles and laughter than most earthly things put together must remind us that it is in the little things that we will find mirth and the mad thrill of childhood. Don't grow old in the spirit, mind and heart. Adulthood sucks.

Keeping aside all spirituality and religious books and philosophies on one side, if you can make somebody smile or gurgle with laughter, you have taken away a bit of load from the shoulders of the Masters and Angels. Spread true joy within and outside. Life is anyway going to kill us one day, but the radiance and fragrance that laughter and joy bring is for eternity, making even the heavens a more mirthful destination.

Just don't do it at the expense of another being. That's not spreading joy. It is spreading rot.

Be blessed always.

To truly engage with the vitality of life, be it in the body or in the spirit dimension, is to be able to find joy in the basics. To be able to see the humour in everything, as life, fate and the Master have a groovy sense of humour.

Spread the true joy within and outside. Life is anyway going to kill us one day, but the radiance and fragrance that laughter and joy bring forth live on for eternity, making even the heavens a more mirthful destination.

13

Samadhi, Nirvana and All That . . .

There is this fascinating news report about a 200-year-old Buddhist monk who was found in a cave in Songino Khairkhan district of Ulan Bator, with his body intact, sitting in the lotus position, covered in cattle skin, and in a state of intense meditative trance. His mummified body stood the test of time and according to Buddhist monks, this 200-year-old monk could still be alive and is in a Samadhi trance state called *Tukdam*.

According to Buddhist philosophy, this state of Samadhi or Tukdam is very close to the state of Nirvana, which is the final merging of the individual soul with the Big Boss or The One, who we call God, Goddess, Creator, Ahura, Shiva, Ram, Kali, Allah, Rab or whatever suits your spiritual inclinations.

So what is this state of Samadhi and what about Nirvana?

For me, Samadhi is a state of self-realization achieved either through the pure Grace of the Guru or through intense spiritual discipline. The realization that you have come from the Great Fire and all that which is embodied in that Great Fire is contained within you, and that the Creator and you are one. It is not intellectual knowledge but the soul's realization of this Oneness.

Nirvana is liberation. Liberation from the cycle of birth and death. Liberation from the churning cesspool of karma. Liberation from one's own stupidity and petty ego. I assume Nirvana means one will never truly come back, as one has merged with The One and has become The One, like how water mixed with milk becomes milk too. Samadhi gives you the self-realization which you can use to come back and serve one and all, and basically get your teeth knocked out by benevolent humanity.

Very often, Zoroastrians make a lamp of rose water, oil and milk . . . the rose water merges with the milk while the oil floats on top, and then they light the lamp. Likewise, in the state of Samadhi, you have realized Oneness but have still not completely lost your identity and become a part of the Oneness. But in the state of Nirvana, you have liberated yourself from your own small self and merged with the Ocean and become the Ocean.

So the state of Samadhi comes first and if pursued further, the state of Nirvana follows.

The Perfect Masters have contained their growth to the state of Samadhi as They want to continue helping those who seek to grow spiritually and become One with the Throb of Creation. The Perfect Masters need to just exhale and They shall dwell in the state of Nirvana, but they don't for some reason. They love us so much that They have kept that final Sigh at bay. This is how much They love us and this is why the Guru is the most revered one in all of Creation. I mean the Real Perfect Master. The Giants. Not the riff-raff dwarfs who go about calling themselves Perfect Masters.

Anyway, enough of my ramblings.

In my interviews with Bapuji for *The Aum Of All Things*, we discussed what the elusive term Samadhi meant.

'Beta, what is this state of Samadhi or Liberation that everybody keeps talking about? The state of Samadhi, according to me, means the real state of the soul. When an individual recognizes one's true state, it gains knowledge of the self or knowledge of the soul. To attain the state of Samadhi, what does the soul have to do? What kind of appropriate action does the soul have to perform? Whatever recording the soul has within itself, all that knowledge the soul will gain. Every soul is different in its state of evolution, even though inherently one. One can go into the state of Samadhi only after following certain procedures, mainly celibacy and yogic breathing. Unless one does not achieve that level of *Brahmacharya* or celibacy, one cannot achieve Samadhi. They say that if one keeps untainted celibacy for twelve long years, is celibate even in the state of dreams, practices pranayama or yogic breathing every day, and chants the sacred word '*Aum*' (or the word he/she believes represents the word God), he/she will awaken the power of the soul which reposes in the Root Chakra or the Muladhar Chakra. When the Muladhar Chakra gets awakened, the energy travels through the other Chakras and reaches the soul.'

Wow! Celibacy and pranayama for twelve years! I think it is safe to say most of us are going to be in the state of non-Samadhi for a really, I mean a really long time!

But to tell you the truth, I don't believe that celibacy has anything to do with spirituality or even Samadhi. Yes, celibacy helps if you are keen on awakening your Kundalini and want to acquire certain paranormal powers. In sex, the very word 'discharge' means something that once had power; through the dissipation of energy, the power gets discharged.

So if you are keen on taking the energy that reposes in the Muladhar Chakra and make the Kundalini Shakti travel through the other Chakras, right up to the Crown Chakra, then yes, it is important that the energy is not discharged via sexual release. But that is if you want to acquire powers or Sidhis. I believe the power of God reposes in the Heart

Chakra, which is well above the naughty Chakra. Thus by being selfless, pure, kind, noble (not stupid, just noble), you will merge with your Master, with or without the use of the libido. God's kingdom is not filled with celibates. It is filled with good people. Heaven is not some exclusive club for vegetarians and celibates. It's packed with honest-to-God, fun-loving, kind-hearted souls who wish well, and who want to spread well-being. So according to me, and I may not be the best person to speak about celibacy and all that, but I know it in my gut that true purity, humility and compassion open wider doors to Oneness, realization and eventually liberation. But for that, one needs to operate from the state of pure, spiritual nothingness, detachment, and selfless compassion and love. It's all about love.

'Where does the soul reside?' I asked Bapuji.

'In the Third Eye or *Ajna* Chakra resides the soul; the point in between the brows on the forehead. When one does *anulom* and *vilom* or alternative nostril breathing as practiced in yogic pranayama, the entire subtle body comes together at one place, which is in the centre point between the brows. Thus, through the practice of celibacy and yogic breathing, the soul remembers its *Ishtu Dev* or one's Primordial God, Goddess or Guru; basically The One he/she prays to. Thus, while doing yogic breathing or pranayama, one has to focus on The One who you believe in and worship. By performing pranayama and the chanting of the 'Aum' sound, all the subtle energies gather into the soul and the soul awakens. That is when the soul experiences the subtle mind and goes into complete silence and the State of Formlessness. Focus on your God or Goddess or Guru, and make sure your mind doesn't stray. After a while, your mind will be truly focused. It will not be able to see anything else but That, and only That, and only That. By focusing on the yogic breathing and The One, whatever power The One will have will get transferred to you. Thus, be careful who you keep your focus on during meditation and pranayama.'

It makes sense. You become who you meditate on. Focus on Baba Sai of Shirdi and all that which He stands for shall be yours too with His Grace. If you meditate on water, you shall encompass the qualities of water and not fire.

'So, when the complete subtle body converges into the soul, the lack of a subtle body within the gross body leaves a vacuum and there is no consciousness of the body. This is when the soul reaches the *Sahastragar*—the ninth Chakra (I assume that this is in the astral body of each individual as the Crown Chakra is the seventh Chakra). In the Sahastragar, there is a cell of each of soul's Creations. In the Sahastragar, there is Godhood. There are cells of innumerable crores of Creations. So in the Samadhi state, the soul experiences the recordings that are already there in the soul and gains self or soul knowledge. So whatever recording is present in the soul is passed on to the individual. As the soul has come from far and above, the knowledge is enlightening.

'The soul will be in the Samadhi *Avastha* or state of Liberation when there is no body consciousness. That is why Gautam Buddha sometimes could not hear any sound, even if you hammered a nail into His ear . . . that is the state of Samadhi. It is when the subtle mind opens up. By staying in the subtle . . . or one can even call this state the Prime Subconscious Mind, the soul becomes totally awakened to its history and potential. There is so much silence that anyone who looks at the individual will assume that the person is dead. The more you move into this state of Samadhi, the soul of that person comes out of the body along with its subtle body. How does this happen? The Dasam Dwar or the tenth door or the tenth Chakra opens. So when the soul comes out, it goes away to roam in its Brahmand or Creation. Where does the soul really go? It can go to the various levels of heaven. If it has more power, then it can travel up to the higher dimensions.

'If you go into the subtle or Prime Subconscious Mind, then you will go beyond the limited mind and the limited bodily relations or blood relations as well. You cannot remember anything related to your daily life when you are at that stage. From the subtle or Prime Subconscious you reach the Prime Unconscious Mind. You are part of the process of Creation. So much energy comes into the soul that you get the speed of the Infinite Mun or the Heart–Mind called '*Bayhud Ke Mun Ki Gati*' or the Speed of Infinite Heart–Mind. There is so much speed as there is so much power.

'But why is the state of Samadhi not so easily reachable? Tell me, beta?'

'Is that a tricky question? I mean, practising celibacy for twelve years and going about life doing alternate nostril breathing! I mean, come on. There has to be a better way to tap into one's subtle or pure subconsciousness, without getting the libido in knots and doing alternative nostril breathing.'

'Naughty boy you are! The reason the state of Samadhi is so elusive is because we are all entangled in the body consciousness—the body and everything that is related with the body and our circle of emotions. Most people see the body and then remember only the body. They immediately come into body consciousness and the whole game is over. What can one do? That is why awakening the pure subconscious mind is so important. One can call the awakening of the subtle mind a state of 'enlightened death' too. The soul goes into such a state of calm silence that we refer to it as death. The process removes the subtle body out and allows the soul to move out of the body. Many of our rishi munis or evolved sages had the knowledge of going out of the body at will. They would travel, gather consciously all the knowledge they wanted and then try to enlighten the world.'

According to me, the more you get into the technicalities of spirituality, the more you realize that heaven and hell are within each one of us; the blossoming of one's true self and the destruction of all that which is true is within oneself. The power to discriminate between right and wrong and the power to choose between the Light or the chaos within is within ourselves. For me, liberation means being free from one's own clutches of darkness and desires, and shedding off the false self and letting one's true self shine through. And it is not easy. The path to liberating yourself from your lower self is filled with spiritual landmines and failures. But you have to keep at it. Fall. Rise. Fall. Rise. Keep at it. Try and try and try to lengthen the moments of Light and prolong the distance between the moments of darkness.

Yes, we are human and yes, we are going to blunder and so we need to try harder to embrace the Light for a little longer. The Light within is elusive; it's playful; it's a lover who wants to be possessed but won't ever surrender till you are worthy. So keep at it and someday, may be lifetimes later, you and I will be worthy of Her and be filled with Her and radiate Her essence and then become One with Her. Just keep at it. Trying to make one's Master happy and proud of you, in spite of falling so many times, is the only dream worth having and till you don't reach it, keep trying. That is the only true purpose of life.

Raising the Kundalini, the state of Samadhi and Nirvana and all that is great, but as Sai Baba of Shirdi often says, there is a difference between Sidhi and Shudhi, which means that there is a difference between spiritual powers and spiritual purity. You may have your Kundalini all awakened and suited and booted, but that gives no guarantee of true spiritual growth. But yearning to be spiritually pure has one guarantee—it's going to tickle the Old Man's funny bone and make Him grin ear-to-ear.

The state of Samadhi is the state of Active Oneness. The state of Nirvana is the Ocean of Bliss. There are idiots who still choose to serve than bask in the glory of Supreme Nothingness.

This for me is worth more than all the Brahmands in all the universes.

Be blessed always.

In the state of Samadhi, you have realized Oneness but have still not completely lost your identity and become a part of the Oneness. But in the state of Nirvana, you have got liberated from your own small self and merged with the Ocean and become the Ocean.

Liberation means being free from one's own clutches of darkness and desires, and shedding off the false self and letting one's true self shine through.

The path to liberating yourself from your lower self is filled with spiritual landmines and failures. But just keep at it. Fall. Rise. Fall. Rise. Keep at it.

True purity, humility and compassion open wider doors to Oneness, realization and eventually liberation.

14

Har Har Mahadev

For me, Lord Shiva is the physical manifestation of our Creator. He is beyond rules. He is beyond laws. He is beyond good and what normal society calls civilized. I mean, who can be called the Lord of all yogis and the creator of yoga, which is about Spirit and Oneness and everything sublime, and also be the creator of *tantra*, which is all about exploring every aspect of oneself, including the physical, in all its raw glory? Both have the same purpose, which is to take you beyond the physical, beyond matter, into the realm of Oneness and Spirit Union, and to merge matter and spirit, making it a throbbing exhalation of Divine Consciousness.

Yoga and tantra are both in His grasp. So is energy and matter. Spirit and body. Sublime and raw passion.

Only Shiva can carry both these vehicles to the final destination, which is eventually to Himself.

There is a poem by Rumi which reminds me of Lord Shiva. It goes something like this, 'Somewhere *beyond* right and wrong, there is a garden. I will meet you there.'

Lord Shiva is beyond prejudices and the conventional mire of morality. He is found roaming in the crematorium, smeared in ash and also in the holy mountain, Kailas or Kailash, deep in meditation. Only He could have made millions worship a phallus seated on a *yoni,* the female genital, a physical representation of Creation; the Male and Female Energy; and the dormant and the active.

Lord Shiva and Goddess Parvati have various stories written about Them and Their Creation and Their Union, but for me, They are the physical manifestations of the Creator. The Creator is neither male nor female but a union of both God and Goddess Energy and the closest resemblance one could dare fathom is that of Ardhanarishvara, which is depicted as one body, but made up of Lord Shiva and Maa Parvati. The Perfect Union of Masculine and Feminine Energy. One without the other is incomplete.

Shiva stands for detachment. He roams about in the crematorium, which is symbolic of the greatest reality, that change is the only constant thing in Creation. One is born and then one passes over to be born again and so on and so forth. To be attached to the temporary is a futile exercise. To give all-pervasive importance to anything attached to the body or the physical is a sign of decay, as all that which is transient will decay one day. Only the Spirit lives on. The only reality is that there is no reality. The existence of The One and the purpose of life is to realize this reality and to move towards it; any by-lane that moves away from this greatest reality is moving away from Lord Shiva.

The only thing permanent is the Spirit—the energy which is housed in the body or the material self or the shell. By roaming either in the crematorium or in the mountains, Shiva makes it clear that the only true form of living is to be detached not just from one's surroundings but most importantly from one's false perception of permanence which is attached to the physical and the material.

According to me, He does not preach to be aloof from the world but to be detached from one's lower self and one's own obsession with the transient nature of the physical and the material. It is easy to be detached from the externals, but one has to be detached from one's own mind, cravings, paranoia, prejudices, pettiness, slander, fears and also from the importance of the ramifications of virtues and vices—if one is good or noble or righteous for any other reason other than for being good and noble and righteous, it then becomes a business and takes us away from the purity of divinity.

When one goes beyond needs, wants, love, lust, hate and most importantly one's own false notion of the self (generally termed as ego; ego does not mean identifying with one's true self but aligning with the transitory and lower self, and all the other fleeting emotions attached to anything which is not permanent), then one begins to tread the path of Shiva. The only thing permanent is The One and one's own higher self, which has come forth from The One.

Everything comes from nothing and goes back to the supreme state of nothingness. Even Creation has come from nothingness and preservation is a necessity of that state of Creation. Creation and preservation need each other, but nothingness needs nothing and is dependent on nothing. Hence it is independent and free from bondage of any sort. The true state of Creation is Divine Nothingness, Divine Darkness and Divine Stillness. But not many can conjure the highest state of Oneness as a state of Divine Darkness or Divine Nothingness. That is why Maa Kali is envisioned as dark in colour. She is the one who kills off all that which takes you away from the ultimate reality and thus She is associated with Darkness, the Divine Darkness.

It is now scientifically proven that space is a state of darkness. Light has come forth from the Creator as to be blissful in that state of nothingness is not meant for one and all. Thus, like a parent who leaves a night bulb on for a child who sleeps in the room alone at night, one has to go even beyond Light into that womb of Divine Darkness to be able to realize his supreme state of detachment.

Thus, Lord Shiva represents detachment and one can only merge with Him when you leave yourself behind and operate from a finality of Oneness.

To be detached from the self is the real answer. We can be a part of the world and still be detached from it; this is possible only if we are detached from our own ego and what we associate ourselves with. Baba Sai in channelling has often said that the final state of detachment is when praise and insult mean the same, as well as the so-called honour and dishonour of one's name.

When love and hate do not ruffle us. When being judged and the need to judge have lost their hold over our ego. When roaming in the crematorium, in the bowels of death or sitting majestically in the Himalayas, deep in meditation, mean the same. When the sky and Mother Earth are both as transitory as dew and thoughts, one begins the true journey to Lord Shiva.

When one goes even beyond the union of energy and matter, power and inertia, honour and dishonour, repute and disgrace, richness and poverty, black and white, even beyond religion and scriptures, that is the time you begin to move towards the Creator—towards Goddess and God Energy, the union of Maa Parvati and Lord Shiva, one body, one form, a union of life and Samadhi, the state of Ardhanarishvara.

Mahashivratri, the most auspicious night dedicated to Lord Shiva, is in reality the union of Lord Shiva and Maa Parvati. When Divine Nothingness had the purpose of Creation, that state of darkness or Big Night became the most auspicious time of all Creation.

Lord Shiva is also called the Destroyer. For me, He destroys the last shreds of ignorance and the false ego or the lower self. Each one of us represents the entire cosmos or Creation. He destroys the false illusions of one's existence, one's cosmos or universe and recreates the real you—the you that swims in the ocean of Oneness and spirit consciousness.

He is the vanquisher of ignorance. In my Fire Temple in Charni Road, Mumbai, there is a board with the sayings of Prophet Zarathustra. I used to read those sayings every day as I lived in the same colony where this beautiful Fire Temple was situated. One statement of the Prophet always confused my daft, young mind. Now the mind is no longer young, but has managed to sustain its remarkable daftness as yet. And for some reason this one saying makes a little more sense. The words are . . . 'There is no greater sin than the sin of ignorance.'

The ignorance spoken about is that of being ignorant of one's own true self and the path that shall lead each one of us, eventually, to that state of wisdom of one's own true self.

To go beyond this trap of ignorance, one reaches out to Lord Shiva. It is through our ignorance that we gravitate to everything that is temporary. It is through the lack of ignorance and the embracing of wisdom that we move towards The One. Shiva is the name of that One for me. Yes, He/She has many names—Ahura Mazda, God, Allah, to name a few. To reach the Divine Union, one needs to go beyond the haze and trap of ignorance. The first step is to be detached from all the false and temporary perceptions and notions. One needs to go within and connect with one's breath, and then through the beautiful streams of the breath and inherent energy to be able to swim in the depths of Oneness and Stillness. It is through Stillness that all doors open——Stillness of one's mind and breath, and Stillness from the ranting and raving of one's mind, false ego and the gravitational pull of the transitory and external. When one achieves this Stillness, then one is able to glimpse Shiva in all His glory.

But for me even the physical manifestation of Shiva is not the ultimate reality and it is that which He wants to teach. Even His physical manifestation as Divine Light is not reality. The reality is to go even beyond His form and symbol and when one does so, it is said that He smiles and embraces you and in less than a sigh and a beat of the heart, you realize that you have become part of Shiva . . . in fact, you have always been Shiva, but a dormant body of hazy consciousness. He makes you go beyond all illusions, to the realization that the Goddess Energy, in the form of the Kundalini, flows within you and your body and its unconscious state of True Consciousness, till now dormant like a corpse. But now with the gushing and merging of the energy, you become Ardhanarishvara yourself and it is then you experience the true essence of the Greatest Union, Mahashivratri.

Be blessed always.

Har Har Mahadev.

Shiva stands for detachment. He roams about in the crematorium, which is symbolic of the greatest reality that change is the only constant thing in Creation.

To go beyond this trap of ignorance, one reaches out to Lord Shiva. It is through our ignorance that we gravitate to everything which is temporary. It is through the lack of ignorance and the embracing of wisdom that we move towards The One. Shiva is the name of that One.

Lord Shiva represents detachment and one can only merge with Him when you leave yourself behind and operate from a finality of Oneness.

The only true form of living is to be detached not just from one's surroundings but from one's false perception of permanence which is attached to the physical and the material.

15

The Path to God Is Merciless

Avatar Meher Baba has taught me the importance of obedience to the Master. I am far from truly following all that He wants us all to comprehend and adhere to but nonetheless, I truly believe that the greatest and the most sublime way to show Him you truly Love Him is by obeying Him and all that which He has taught, with complete soul surrender. My understanding of Him is simple. First comes obedience; obedience is the greatest expression of love to the Master. Without obedience one cannot claim selfless love or complete surrender to the Master.

I remember reading extracts from *Lord Meher*, the detailed biography of Avatar Meher Baba, where His most intimate disciples have jotted down minute details of their life with the Avatar. What comes through is the complete surrender of His disciples or the inner circle or the *mandali* to Meher Baba.

There were times His behaviour was inexplicable. Very often even contradictory. Sometimes even exasperating. One thing was clear, if you wanted to truly love Him, you had to completely surrender and to prove one's inherent surrender, one had to live a life of exacting obedience.

He would spend months working on a project and He would insist that the work was of utmost importance. Let us say, construction of a hospital or school. The disciples would slog night and day, amidst the most exacting of conditions. Nearing completion, He would smile and say that the work has been completed from the spirit or astral or causal point of view and the place would either be demolished or abandoned.

Those who loved Him knew He had His divine reasons, He knew best and He was always right. Those who assumed they loved Him would question Him or grumble or get exasperated. Some would leave. Some would begin to have doubts. It was only those who had a vague or certain belief of His Godhood who would exhale and say 'Jai Baba'.

Meher Baba, like all Masters, was different with His inner circle or disciples and with those who sought Him for His blessings or solutions to their everyday problems. With the latter, those who went about life like normal people——work, family, friends and a part of their heart devoted to the Avatar—— were treated tenderly, with a smile, and with a large helping of humour. If they did falter, Meher Baba would be like a father who would calmly explain their failings and weaknesses to them and tenderly nudge them towards the right path. Where His devotees were concerned, He, according to me, did not expect complete obedience or surrender. He was aware of their spiritual journey and thus their spiritual potential, and happy to receive whatever love, surrender and obedience was possible, depending upon each one's spiritual inclination and potential. No mistake was unpardonable. There was always a pat on the back and He would tenderly implore them to be on the path.

The biographies or songs or tales of miracles, where the Master is described as an affable Santa Claus, is mainly for devotees. For them, the Master, God, Goddess or Avatar is one part of the five-course meal. It could be the main dish, side dish or the dessert. For those fortunate folks, like all Masters, Meher Baba took on the role of a gentle Spiritual Giant.

What most biographies, tales, myths, songs and miracles very often avoid mentioning is how the Master or Avatar behaves with His/Her inner circle or mandali.

Meher Baba was full of love and humour, but He could appear brutal when He saw even one of them slipping a bit from the path. His logic, I assume, was simple. If you come to Him as a devotee, all smiles and seeking favours or help, you would get a tender Master, smiling and blessing you, and making you feel good about yourself. He would help you bear the burden of your karmic blueprint and tenderly nudge you to keep moving on the path.

But if by mistake you proclaimed that you had completely surrendered to Him——your logic, your emotions, your passions, your weaknesses, your fears, your life and most importantly your very soul——then He had only one duty towards you and that was to clean you off all the karmic baggage and garbage clinging to your aura. He had to make sure that you merged into Him; your life, then and beyond, was for Him to decide.

Even the small mistakes of those few disciples were dealt with so harshly that made even Hitler seem like a genial schoolmaster who had a slight issue with one sect of the population.

As Baba Sai says so often, 'You cannot be partially pregnant; one is either pregnant or not pregnant.' Similarly, Meher Baba said, 'If you call me your Lord and Master, then you shall do as I tell you. Keep your thinking and ego to yourself. I have no place for it. If you want *moksha* and believe I am the One who can release you from the cycle of births and deaths, karma and its ramifications, then just obey. If you believe I am your way out, then follow Me with full faith and not a question on your lips or in your hearts.'

I believe it was Meher Baba who said that God is all merciful but the path to God is merciless. And oh boy, He did prove this phrase right.

He made you understand the ferocity of walking the path to God.

Where His disciples were concerned, there was only one rule. Obey, obey and obey. Love and surrender were the pillars and foundation, but obedience was the path to the heart of the Avatar, our Meher Baba.

He could be merciless when He felt one of His own straying away from the path. He knew the path of each one and thus He was clear how to steer each one towards the final destination and merger. The True Masters and Avatars know it all. They are Giants. If you follow a Giant, He/She will clear the path you tread on. Leave it all to the Giant to navigate you through the rigmarole of your karmic and mundane life.

There was an incident I read about Meher Baba. He once asked one of His disciples to cook a particular dish for Him. He told her to do nothing else but focus on preparing the dish as He, since some time, had been craving to eat this particular dish prepared by her. The disciple was overjoyed.

So this woman, overjoyed to be cooking for her Master or Avatar or God, began to prepare the dish to the best of her ability, with all concentration and love. She spent a long time getting everything ready and then slowly, with love brimming in her heart, she began to prepare the meal. Suddenly, if I remember correctly, a fire broke out in the ashram. Many were hurt. So she put out the fire (in those days they didn't have gas cylinders or pipeline gas; they would mostly cook on wooden logs) and rushed to help those who were hurt. In some time, everything was back to normal and she returned to prepare the dish. The meal was ready and she was happy, but she was apprehensive if it would please her Master and Avatar.

Meher Baba came and sat down to eat. He took a morsel, then chucked the plate and walked away. The woman was heartbroken and inconsolable. She could not fathom His behaviour. Even if the dish was not palatable, she knew that Meher Baba would eat it. She could not believe her cooking was so bad that it had infuriated her Master to such an extent that He had done something He had never ever done before——reject food in such a violent manner.

After some time or few hours or days, I do not remember too clearly, she found herself in front of Meher Baba. He looked at her and explained to her the reason for His behaviour. He had asked her to prepare Him a dish. Did He ask her to put out the fire? Nope. If she believed Him to be either her Master or Avatar or God, then her duty and her dharma was to only focus on preparing the meal for Him. How the hell did it matter if there was a fire or an earthquake or the dissolution of the world? If she truly loved Him, then she should have given her undivided attention to the task or request made to her by her Avatar and Master.

Even if the roof were to fall on her, she should have gone about preparing the meal, and if she had to succumb doing so, it shouldn't have mattered. He had not rejected the food. He had rejected her disobedience. He had told her before leaving that she should do nothing else but prepare the food. Putting out the fire was not a part of His command. He then smiled and asked her if she could, for God's sake, now prepare the dish and do nothing else but prepare it.

Remember, this entire incident seen from another context or through the eyes of a layman might make Meher Baba seem like a dictator or a person throwing an attitude. It was not so. For Him, it was all about 'not respecting His word', as first came the word and from it came about everything.

When you truly surrender to your Master, first and foremost you surrender the ego, the mind and the lower self. Without doing this, all love is meaningless; it is then directed mainly towards yourself, rather than to your Master. If the Master tells you it is night and in reality it is midday, then too there is a reason. The only one who truly loves will not only accept that it is night, but believe it too. You might call it blind faith, but faith is anything but blind. Faith sees what the eyes cannot behold. It sees beyond the three dimensions. It sees through the eyes of the Master.

Mehera Maa loved Her Avatar so much that She knew what He wanted of Her, even before He voiced it aloud. This kind of love comes forth from complete surrender, where obedience becomes the very exhale and sigh of one's soul. It is not just obeying but obeying with happiness, grace and joy.

This, I believe, is what Meher Baba wanted to truly make one and all understand. It is not easy to live with true Masters. They are not interested in what you think of Them, but only what They want to make out of you. Sai Baba of Shirdi so often said, when in His body and also during channelling, that 'Till you do not understand you and I are One, our journey has not even begun.' To understand Oneness, you should begin with complete, pure, dog-like surrender and obedience. Everything else is shadow-boxing.

Be blessed always.

Where His disciples were concerned, there was only one rule. Obey, obey and obey. Love and surrender were the pillars and foundation, but obedience was the path to the heart of the Avatar, our Meher Baba.

When you truly surrender to your Master, first and foremost you surrender the ego, the mind and the lower self. Without doing this, all love is meaningless; it is then directed mainly towards yourself, rather than to your Master.

16

When Being Spiritual Can Be Unspiritual

The fact is that there is no one particular path to reach God, Goddess and Guru. There are innumerable ways, beautiful by-lanes, various peaks and valleys and if you keep on walking calmly and with pure love from within for The One, you will reach your destination. When and how is karmic, but what goes beyond karma too is one's yearning to breathe in deep the *khushboo* or the divine fragrance. If the need is all-pervasive, not even your own destiny's blueprint can prevent you from reaching the Old Chap with that vague music sense.

Nobody can give you directions regarding this journey. It is your flight and in all probability, the scenery and the road may not have been traversed by anybody before you.

You can read about the travels of others and how they reached their destination to avoid certain terrains and climates, to know where to halt and where to refuel, where to eat and stay or not eat and run for your life. You can read accounts of countless such road trips. But eventually, you might never steer your vehicle on that particular road and all you have read and memorized would mean nothing. Nothing you have read and been cautioned about or encouraged for will matter as the damn pathway is different. Even the seasons might differ and the intensity of the season might be completely off the barometer.

This is your path. This is about you and your God, Goddess and Guru. I can keep harping on till I develop a third kidney but all I talk to you about is my reality. It may not be your reality. Thus my blabber is only for those who are taking the same route I have. It would make sense to know the stuff I have witnessed, but my path may have innumerable by-lanes and you might choose another by-lane, and everything I have witnessed might no longer be applicable as you are now on a terrain which nobody has written about.

The problem is not that there are innumerable roads leading to The One but that most people are certain that their pathway is the only true approach to liberation, heaven, God, Goddess and Guru.

This gives birth to a divide and mankind's history is a testimony of the senseless bloodshed that has taken place in the name of God and religion. The sad reality is that there have been more wars fought in the name of God than in the name of the devil. The devil, the lucky bastard, has to do nothing but smoke a joint, scratch his privates, belch and see mankind destroy itself and make the heavens weep.

The only reality about liberation, moksha and all this spiritual orchestra is that there are innumerable ways of reaching The One. I read somewhere that Lord Buddha had told His disciples that just as there are countless ways of meditation, similarly there are myriad ways of reaching the Big Boy.

Time and again I have mentioned in books, blogs and in videos that indulging in charity and helping those less fortunate than you is one of the easiest and most sublime ways of pleasing the Grumpy One. You can then be assured of reaching your spiritual destination and even attaining liberation via prayers and meditation.

The sad fact is that even here people seem to have taken the act of compassion and the time spent in prayer and meditation as a means to prove one's superiority, and in some way or the other make the rest feel less spiritual.

We are so spiritually bankrupt that we somehow can take the most sublime act and smear it with our self-centredness and insistence for self-glorification. I have known people who will throw it in your face about how kind, generous and charitable they are, and how often they meditate and pray, for self-glorification and also in a way to put the other person down. This is akin to preparing an elaborate meal for one's Master and then pissing on it.

Of course, there are people who will slander those who are genuinely kind-hearted and charitable, and also those who are truly immersed in prayer and meditation. We are like crabs that pull down anyone just about to get out of captivity. Most often it is about 'I-me-myself'.

Many times I have been told by friends that maybe they are not spiritual or blessed as they neither have the means for indulging in charity and helping others nor do they have the time for prayers and meditation due to their circumstances. It does not help that others have tried their level best to flaunt either their financial generosity or hours spent in prayer and meditation.

The question to ask is what happens if you do not have the resources to go all out and indulge in sharing your wealth with the less financially fortunate? Or if you do not have the time or the circumstances to be able to pray for long or meditate for more than maybe a few minutes? Does that mean you are not as spiritual as those who have the money to help others or the means, time and environment to spend time in prayers and meditation?

I never really imagined that there were people who were grappling with an inferiority complex because Holy Books or sermons or writings kept drubbing it into their heads that the more you indulge in charity, prayers and meditation, the more spiritual you become——a cut above the 'mango people' or the *aam admi*, the true common man. The doubt that 'Maybe I am not doing enough to qualify as a spiritual person or somebody dear to God as I do not have the means or circumstances for charity and prayers' seems to be bothering more people today.

I have often been told that so and so is a very pious man or woman as he/she helps the less fortunate with time and money or spends hours in prayers and contemplation, indirectly hinting that they or I are not in the league of these spiritually enhanced people due to our inability to indulge in charity or prayers to such an extent.

I do not have an answer to what pleases God. I barely know the Unshaven One. All I do know is I am deeply flawed, but with all my flaws, there is still deep love for Him/Her. Also if I am flawed, it is for no other reason but due to my own failings and weaknesses at different points in time. Nothing to do with God, Goddess and Guru, and the lack of charity, prayers or meditation. I do not believe God or anything outside me has any role to play in me being such a monumental dork and no amount of prayers, meditation and indulging in charity is going to change my inherent self. It is this inherent self that shall decide when and how I reach my final destination of being face to face with The One and sort of tickle His/Her funny bone. Who I am is going to decide my true destination and not what I do or not do.

I may pray for hours, all through the day, but if in those hours while am not praying I do not live as a decent human being, compassionate to the pain, suffering and circumstances of those around me, of what good are my hour-long prayers? No matter with what intensity or purity I might pray. It will not matter. And if I cannot make my life a living prayer, nothing else matters. It is not just my time spent in prayer but also my time when I make my life either a living prayer or a living hell for those around me that decides on which side of the spiritual barometer I truly stand.

Yes, it would be beautiful if I could pray and also live a life that makes my God, Goddess and Guru happy and proud of me. That would be truly beautiful and it is this aspect of my life which shall decide how truly spiritual I am, not the hours spent in prayers. What matters is the time spent not in prayer, by operating from being soul conscious and not body conscious.

I have known atheists who are far more spiritual than those who spend hours in prayers. Even if the atheist does not believe in God, I am certain that God believes and respects the atheist, for he/she has made his/her life into a prayer, by behaving in a manner that makes the Great Flame brighter by reflecting the glory, radiance and fragrance of his/her Source. Even if that person does not believe in that Source, it truly doesn't matter.

It is important to pray, but it is a million times more important to make your life a prayer.

For me, charity or helping those in need is a sublime way of making life into a living prayer. How much you are able to do will depend upon your circumstances and your inclination. A man who can donate a million, and does donate a million, is doing so because his/her circumstance permits the individual to do so. Great. It is a beautiful gesture to be able to donate money or kind and spread happiness, comfort and compassion to the most needy.

But if you do charity to make yourself feel good, noble, more spiritual or to prove a point to someone or pamper your ego through the means of comparison, then you have really not got the lyrics of the Great Song. Prayers, meditation and charity should be a way of life, for that is the right way of life. Not because it gains you spiritual brownie points. Then it is just business. And God is a lousy businessman.

Also, you may not have enough money to help others. Does that make you less spiritual? Is it not your primary duty to first take care of your home? I believe it is. Charity begins at home. Do your bit for your family and if there is something left, do the needful for those who are in need. Every small act of kindness helps people and the energy attached to it carries on for eons.

Charity need not be just about money. It is not true that only big bucks can help others. You can be a kind individual. An understanding person. A compassionate idiot. Help someone selflessly. All these things are equally important to spread the Light. It is not always about money. It is about what comes about by sharing money or your time or just a smile or a packet of biscuits with a hungry child or animal, or offering water to someone who is thirsty.

Sometimes a glass of water can save a person's life and at other times, an ocean might not be enough to quench the thirst of a bird.

Do not assess everything based on whether it makes God happy, wins you brownie points or whatever. We need to do what we can do. We need to light candles. If there is one lit candle, even the thickest darkness does not stand a chance.

Yes, it is great if you have the finances and you go all out and help the needy. And it would be better if you have not only helped those in need but is also inherently a good human being. You refrain from slander, gossip and the other equally repellent dark forces. Very often, all a person might need is a smile and a kind word to get the strength to go on with life. All the money in the world might not help over here, but your smile and kind words might change the mind of an individual from ending his/her miserable life. Is that not the greatest prayer or act of charity? I think it is. It financially amounts to nothing and no time is spent in meditation and prayer, but that one smile can save a life.

Who is to judge who is more spiritual than the other? God does not judge. If God does judge, then He/She is no God of mine. My God is not a human being with feathers attached to the posterior and a funny halo around His/Her fat head. My God is cool, loving, peaceful, joyous and understanding, and doesn't ever judge anyone knowing each one is on his/her own journey. Everyone is eventually going to merge with Him/Her and most importantly filled with compassion and largeness of heart. He/She does not need anything from you or me. All we do for Him/Her is for our own selves. We are spiritual or kind or whatever because that is the way we are supposed to be. We are not doing anybody a favour by being decent or by indulging in charity, prayers or meditation. If anybody is the biggest gainer, it is the individual. Not God. God does not need anything, not even our spirituality. May be He/She needs our true love. Love for the sake of love. No give and take. No conditions to apply.

For me, that is the greatest spiritual gift you can give yourself and your God, Goddess and Guru. Come from a place of love, operate from the place of love. Become a throbbing, radiant, fragrant being of love. When you reach that stage, you do not have to do anything. Your very presence will uplift all around you and give a beautiful nudge to all of Creation to walk the path.

Sometimes feeding a tired, mangy dog a packet of biscuits can be the most meaningful act of spirituality. Do not judge yourself for what you are not, but for what you are.

Spread the Light. Spread the joy. Spread the love. Everything else is shadow-boxing.

> *It is important to pray, but it is a million times more important to make your life a prayer.*
>
> *Come from a place of love, operate from the place of love. Become a throbbing, radiant, fragrant being of love. When you reach that stage, you do not have to do anything. Your very presence will uplift all around you and give a beautiful nudge to all of Creation to walk the path.*
>
> *If there is one lit candle, even the thickest darkness does not stand a chance.*

17

Silence Is a Strange Animal

Iknow I have talked and written about the importance of silence, but I believe that one needs to be careful of the kind of silence one practices.

Silence is a strange animal and like all animals, silence too comes in various sizes and shapes. It is safe to say that silence can often create more emotional, physical, mental and spiritual wreckage than all the noise in the world.

Silence can be akin to numbness. It may seem to be insulating you from further harm, but in reality, it is like cancer that spreads deep into your very consciousness, making you impotent of feeling, thinking and being proactive rather than reactive.

Many use silence as a tool of survival. But that very contrivance can become like quicksand.

Very often silence can be louder than words.

Thus, it is important to understand the true meaning of silence that all Masters, scriptures and now a dork like me keep insisting upon.

When I talk about silence, I talk about a state of stillness within. A state of positive acceptance. A peaceful consciousness. Immersing yourself in the moment and becoming the moment after a while. All this may sound like spiritual mumbo jumbo, but you, my demented friend, need to give being in the moment a try, and you will begin to get my nonsensical drift. Silence is not golden. Silence is more precious than all the trinkets put together. You will find yourself, your true being, your real priorities and maybe even catch a whiff of the other side in the calm stillness, centredness or state of silence.

You can talk all day and yet be in a state of stillness and positive silence within, or you can stop talking to the world but be in a state of noise within.

Once again, I am not talking about the state of void, emptiness, aloofness or forced detachment that is a shield from getting hurt. Nor am I talking about it as the only weapon to fight back whoever is trying to skin you metaphorically or indulging in it due to not having a choice or due to fear.

All this looks like silence. Feels like silence. But the good Lord riding a bicycle knows that this isn't silence. This is a state of suppressed rage or sadness and this zone in reality is a state of cacophony and noise so loud it leads to physical illness, emotional bitterness, mental depression and spiritual bankruptcy.

When I began to wander aimlessly in the world of the paranormal, I was told very clearly, by some voice——I would like to believe that was the voice of my Master, but you could just go about assuming it to be some schizophrenic blabber within me——that the path towards becoming a medium, channel or an instrument who communicates with the other side, the other dimension, begins, grows and matures in the state of calm silence.

And I said, 'Yeah, right' to either my Master or my state of schizophrenic jabber within.

So the first step was to be in the moment for forty days and nights. Which meant, if I was eating, then I should do nothing but be in the moment of eating. Let me tell you, the food began to taste more unpalatable as my cook was first a plumber in the hinterlands of India and had come to settle all karmic baggage with me.

If I was watching a movie, I had to watch the blasted movie. If I was bathing, then I should be in the process of cleaning my battered body. Be it smoking, drinking, working, praying or whatever, one had to be in that moment.

And what does all this absolute nonsense achieve? In reality, it achieves nothing.

As my Master, Sai Baba of Shirdi says so often during channelling and in my prayer: the true state of being is to be in the state of nothingness.

This state of nothingness is a zone where you are so immersed in the darned moment that after a while you become the moment. When you become the moment, you begin to get acquainted with your higher self or your Guides or your Masters or may be a calmer, cooler, schizophrenic you.

Slowly the mind gets calmer. You are in control. You think when you want to. It is like actually giving your mind the permission to think. The horses called emotions and thoughts are under your reins now. You know where to take the bastards. You will come to a point where you will give yourself permission to be in the moment of sorrow, stress or anger. You will take time out and tell yourself, 'Okay, you lousy dork, I give you half an hour for all your miserly moping and groaning. After that, get on with your life.'

And after that given time, you will exhale and get back to giving yourself to the moment and in that moment, you will find calm silence.

Silence is a state of being cool on the highway of life. This silence means a state of not reacting to the stimulus around you.

Trust me, we have ample opportunities to react but when you are in the state of calmness or silence, or in the moment, your reaction time will start getting slower, and then as though on a perpetual high——this high is that of stillness——you will let your consciousness focus on things that matter rather than on things that slowly kill you——physically, emotionally or worse, spiritually.

Silence, the true kind, is not an excuse or some state of self-defence against anger, hate, fear or life. Nope. That is not silence but noise gone wrong. You get my drift, don't you? Obviously reading my article does not necessarily speak highly of your state of evolvement, but I hope you get my rambling.

I believe that first came God or should I dare say that God was, is and always will be present? God was silent and may be because of this God was considered to belong to the male species and thereby referred to as a 'He'.

Anyway, the first sound according to the sages was the sound of the word 'Aum'. According to the rishi munis and the Masters, Aum is the sigh of the cosmos; it is the sound of the universe dancing by itself.

Aum or Ahun, as pronounced by Zoroastrians, who belong to the first and the oldest religion known to mankind, is thus the first word. This word, which has originated from the womb of silence, is so powerful that just chanting it has taken scores of seekers to the beyond and back. If the sound of silence can be so powerful, then imagine what power must reside in silence and when one goes even beyond silence to the very Source.

Silence is so supreme that it is through it that the word Aum or Ahun came forth and thus it is in silence that one experiences Oneness and connects to the Oneness Family. It is when you go beyond thought and emotion that you reach the dimension of silence, as both thought and emotion are noises——one of intent and the other of emotion——and action is the culmination of sound of either intent or emotion. That is why Prophet Zarathustra based His philosophy on good thoughts, good words and good deeds.

So first came silence. True silence brought forth noble thoughts. Noble thoughts gave words to the intent and thus came about good words. Hence with calm silence comes good thoughts, which gives birth to good words and eventually good deeds follow.

One of the first times I saw the effect of calm silence or stillness was once when I got a call from a medium and friend at night. She informed me that her sixteen-year-old niece had gone missing. The streets of Mumbai could be merciless to a sixteen-year-old and she wanted me to ask Baba Sai of Shirdi when her niece would be back.

Now the person speaking to me on the phone was a medium too. People went to her for help from all over the country. But it is common knowledge that this breed or species, who claim to have some direct line with spirits, Masters, Angels and all the paranormal stuff, never truly trust themselves with the answers they get about themselves or their lot. The reason is that they are too attached to the situation and when that happens, the state of stillness or silence gets affected. It is the medium's subconscious mind that will come to play and one can never be sure if the message is coming from an unemployed spirit or oneself.

I told my friend that I had got very deeply connected with a certain gentleman called Old Monk and thus I was not the best person to guide her or call on Baba Sai to help her find her missing niece. I was drunk for God's sake. One does not mess around with the other side while being drunk.

And I distinctly remember a voice so loud within my head that I nearly dropped the phone.

'You worm, who predicts, you or I?'

'You predict.'

'If I am the One, I can assure you, I am not drunk. Tell the child that the niece will return home in an hour and not to call the police.'

So I very hesitatingly told my friend that her psychotic niece would return by eleven at night. And that is exactly what happened.

I have been told often that if one is in a state of calm silence, one becomes more receptive to inspiration and intuition. The chap who took off stark nude screaming 'Eureka' is a perfect example.

I can write about silence and what it does to the astral and causal body. I can write about how one's karmic debt can be paid through silence. But that is all spiritual gobbledygook.

If you want to achieve your own potential, you need to befriend yourself. The easiest and surest way is to operate from and live in a state of stillness and silence.

Be blessed.

> *Silence is not golden. Silence is more precious than all the trinkets put together. In the calm stillness, centredness or state of silence you will find yourself, your true being, your real priorities and maybe even catch a whiff of the other side.*
>
> *Silence is so supreme that it is through silence the word 'Aum' or 'Ahun' came forth and thus it is in silence that one experiences Oneness and connects to the Oneness Family.*
>
> *If you want to achieve your own potential, you need to befriend yourself. The easiest and surest way is to operate and live from a state of stillness and silence.*

18

The Spiritual Dwarfs

Every time we judge somebody, slander another being or speak ill of a person, we dwell in the valley of spiritual darkness. We digress from our path and create obstacles for our own growth, and exhibit a beautiful and an undisputable mark of our lack of common sense.

Every individual is a cesspit and a mishmash of varied things.

Each one of us is an amalgamation of so many diverse influences affecting our lives. We have our past-life karma that determines so many things about us and which varies from individual to individual.

Then we have a unique gene pool and DNA. Added to the above two is one's upbringing, which includes family environment, teachers, friends, lovers and financial influences.

Then comes one's inherent tendencies. Of course, the society in which we live, the freedom or restrictions accorded, the level of maturity of the world around us——all this determines how one reacts to family and peer pressure, and every little action, thought and word.

Thus each one of us has so many forces determining how each one thinks, speaks, behaves, acts and reacts to every situation, every moment and every stimulus that life keeps offering or littering one's path with.

The first and most important deciding factor of our individuality, according to me, is one's karmic blueprint and journey. Each one of us is different in our own way and thus we handle each moment in our own individual way, very often not having control of what we do or how we do things—as the genesis of how we behave very often lies in the womb of our past lives.

Why is it that the siblings in one family are so very different? As children, each one of them has had the same environment and upbringing. They have the same gene pool, educational opportunities, financial background, diet, acquaintances, similar platforms or burdens—parallel life patterns in every way. One may be kind and generous, the other a son of a bitch and the third somewhere in between. One may be intelligent but lazy, the other hardworking but not as clever, and the third as wise as a rusted lamp post. One may be honest, the other an opportunist and the third could give a politician an inferiority complex in manipulation and deceit.

Why is each one so different? Everything is similar, but each one is so unlike the other. What happened? If one believes that it is the upbringing and home environment that makes a child, then how come each of the three siblings is so different?

What is it that can make siblings so dissimilar? The answer can be traced to their karmic blueprint and journey—the experiences each one has come to embrace, the rewards to be earned and the price to be paid for things done in the past. Each one is a baffling combination of all our past actions, thoughts, words and deeds. All this determines 90 per cent of who we are and become.

A few days ago, somebody asked me why one particular individual was such an angry human being despite the fact that he prayed all day, was generous and compassionate, and reasonably good. He was a terribly angry soul.

The family members were all calm and composed people, and did not react to situations, while our man could fight even the wind.

The answer lay in the person's karmic past; it may be that in this lifetime he has to go beyond anger. Thus, no matter how much he indulges in prayer, meditation and charity, and comes from love and humaneness, life is going to test him, egg him on and needle him at every given opportunity, to see how he is doing with the anger issue.

Anger was the main agenda in the man's karmic blueprint and memorandum of understanding. May be our man had been grappling with the issue of anger for lifetimes and thus till he did not go beyond the state of anger, he would keep coming back, his nose rubbed more and more into the ground, till the daft dork made a resolve to go beyond anger. He would be tested and tested and tested. He would either be in a state of anger or in a state trying to control his anger.

To judge this individual would be an exercise of large-hearted, dim-witted stupidity as who knows, this dork may have taken this decision to evolve further spiritually. Being able to control our anger is one of the most sublime proofs of spiritual growth as when one can control one's time for reaction or anger, it shows one dwelling in the depths of centredness.

So what I am rambling about is that if you judge an individual, either you have reached a level of phenomenal spiritual heights where you can read a person's karmic blueprint, past, present and future or you have nothing better to do than bitch like a blistering open wound oozing with pus.

Thus, the first thing that determines our mental, emotional and physical tendencies lies in our karmic blueprint, which is not even accessible to the individual, leave aside to factious strangers. So shut the fug up and stop judging and slandering others.

Then comes one's genetic pool bank. Our ancestors have a huge impact on our actions, words and even thoughts. They have a hold on us emotionally, physically and mentally. I had a close friend who had a habit of taking a fish bone and using it as a toothpick. Yes, he was Zoroastrian——a true-blooded *bawa*——and we are, if nothing else, extremely innovative in displaying our levels of ingenuity and madness. My friend's dad had passed over when he was barely a few months old. Since then, my friend had begun to eat fish on his own without chocking himself to death. He would take the fish bone and use it as a toothpick—a habit that he had picked up from his father who did the very same thing. But my friend was not even ninety days old when his father was given a pair of wings.

Imagine, if genetics can have such an influence on even the most bizarre traits, then how deeply must we be influenced by our ancestors in the more important things that construct our personality? That is why ancestors and ancestral worship was such a big thing in the past.

How much credit or blame can we take for our own individuality——stuff like honesty, violence, anger, jealousy, spiritual growth or immaturity and the way we react or act? Is there anything called individuality? Am I daft or intelligent because of my efforts or because of my gene pool, my karma, my upbringing or everything that has influenced me, troubled me or touched me? Now imagine judging somebody? On what basis?

After karma and ancestors come upbringing, schooling, opportunities or lack of them, childhood abuse and experiences, financial platforms or hardships and then the society we live in.

How progressive or regressive it can possibly be. Our teachers, our friends, our lovers, their families, their lawyers . . . the list goes on.

To judge, slander, bitch, gossip, mock, ridicule and basically have a moronic and myopic opinion about everybody shows one's spiritual hypocrisy, intellectual bankruptcy, emotional darkness and immaturity.

When we judge or slander, we light fires under our feet and after a while we feel the flames burning us.

Baba Sai of Shirdi would say that those who gossip and slander are like pigs who feed on their own excreta. Imagine we are feeding on piss, puss and shit every time we indulge in slander and gossip. If that is not good enough for us to stop, I wonder what else is.

We teach our children that stealing is a sin and so is lying, but guess what, bitching and tearing another person to smithereens with one's words or thoughts and ridicule is equally, if not more, a sin. You are indulging in lying, putting somebody down, mocking his/her entire karmic journey, upbringing and circumstances just for a few laughs.

When we judge, we steal the person's respect, we lie about the individual, we destroy the person's image and all that he/she stands for. I would think that accounts for sinning or making God, Goddess and Guru hop around mad with sadness and rage.

Be careful as the one you judge, slander or bitch about may be a pure soul. Trust me, you do not want to mess with a pure soul. The consequences that the cosmos dishes out to those who slander a pure soul are not something I would recommend anyone to go through. Also, who knows, that individual one is mocking and tearing up may be one's greatest well-wisher in the larger scheme of things. Somebody who could have helped you for lifetimes. One never knows. One just does not get to know till it is too late.

I write this as I see around me so much pettiness in the form of everybody playing holier than thou and judging, slandering, mocking and bitching. It makes my very soul want to shrivel up and press the delete button to existence.

Some dork once said that mankind was created in the image of God. Yeah, right. If that is true, you can keep your God.

Be blessed.

> *To judge, slander, bitch, gossip, mock, ridicule and basically have a moronic and myopic opinion about everybody shows one's spiritual hypocrisy, intellectual bankruptcy, emotional darkness and immaturity.*
>
> *When we judge, we steal the person's respect, we lie about the individual, we destroy the person's image and all that he/she stands for.*
>
> *Tearing another person to smithereens with one's words or thoughts and ridicule is equally, if not more, a sin as here you are indulging in lying, putting somebody down, mocking his/her entire karmic journey, upbringing and circumstances just for a few laughs.*
>
> *Each one of us is different in our own way and thus we handle each moment in our own individual way; the genesis of how we behave very often lies in the womb of our past lives.*

19

Godspeed Mom

My mother passed over a couple of years ago. She had brain cancer and slipped into a coma at home, and Baba carried her away to His abode. I was not physically present when both my parents passed away. I guess that does not say much about me as a son.

I have learnt a few things from my mother as I am sure each one of you has from your near and dear ones.

Before I go about rambling about my mother, I need to write a bit on her. My grandmother was born in Iran and arrived in India when she was barely a year old. She came along with her elder sister, who was two years older than her and a brother who was in his late teens. My great grandad used to export dry fruits to India and when he fell ill, the doctors advised him to leave for India for better medical help.

So the parents and three kids arrived in India. The medical treatment failed and my great granddad passed over in Mumbai a few months after they arrived. It was decided that my grand-uncle would go to Iran, liquidate all the business and return to India, where they would settle down amongst the then considerable Zoroastrian and Iranian community.

He was barely out of his teens. He embraced his mother and his two young sisters, climbed on to the boat and left for Iran. That was the last time he was seen by his loved ones. He never reached Iran. Something took place at sea and he passed away, and his body was released into the womb of the Water Goddess. Nobody knows what really took place. Whether he died of natural causes, accident or murder is still left to conjecture even after nearly a hundred years of his passing away.

My great-grandmother went into a state of shock and lost her mental balance. Her two young daughters were given up for adoption and spent a considerable amount of time in Pune, where they used to play with Avatar Meher Baba. She had just begun to recover when one day she sat in a local train, shut her eyes, began to pray and then never opened her eyes ever again.

My grandmother was barely twelve or thirteen when she was married to a young, hot-headed man living in Hyderabad or Secunderabad. He was the only heir of a very wealthy man, with a huge palace-like home and large estate.

When she was barely thirteen or fourteen, she became pregnant. One night, her hot-headed husband had a spat with his father and in the middle of the night, he, along with his young pregnant wife, left the huge house, the vast estate, lots of hard cash and never looked back. I really mean he never looked back. He walked away and nobody knows what happened to the huge house and the damn estate.

So my grandmother, who was born into a wealthy family and married into a wealthier family, for some reason, had a strange karmic connect with hardship and grappling with the callous hands of poverty.

My mother was one amongst seven siblings. My grandfather worked and supported the family while my grandmother took care of the children and home. To supplement the meagre income, she cooked and packed tiffins for a paltry amount. My grandfather, a tough, hot-tempered man, was in love with his first daughter. She would wait for him every night and would help remove his shoes, place his slippers, wait till he washed up and then have dinner with him.

When she was seven or eight years old, she fell and hurt the back of her head while playing. Two nights later, she died in the arms of my grandfather. A man who could take on seven men and come out whistling performed the last rites of not only his daughter but of himself too, as after that he became harsh, violent and ruthless as the very reason of his existence had been wiped out.

My mother often told me that when he came back from work, all the kids would be told to stand in line. He would talk to each one—ask them about their day and the marks they scored, and if there was a slip, the belt would be brought out and the kid senselessly whipped. It was as though a part of him hated the kids to be alive when the throb of his heart, his daughter, had died. What if she had lived and one of the others had died? All this, of course, is my armchair two-bit psychoanalysis.

So, my mother lived amongst four sisters and a brother, a mother who was still a young girl, many dogs, and a father who was like a walking dead man.

My mother was a beautiful woman. She excelled in studies and sports. Everybody was certain her future would be luminous, and she would make a name for herself and make her family proud.

She usually stood first in her class and by the time she appeared for her Class X exams, she had decided that she wanted to become a doctor. She was one of the most compassionate human beings I have ever known. She was fearless, intelligent and cool.

They shifted to Mumbai when her Class X results were declared and her father called her up from Hyderabad to tell her that she had failed. My mother's world collapsed. How could she fail? A student who excelled all her life in sports and studies could just not fail. But her father maintained that she had failed.

Completely disillusioned, my mother decided to no longer pursue her education. To help her mother and siblings begin a new life in Mumbai, she took up a job in the pharmaceutical company, Pfizer. She was barely sixteen years old then.

It was only after a few years that she got to know the truth that she had stood first in the entire state. But her father decided that as he would not be able to support the educational dreams of the rest of the children, it would be best to let my mother assume she had failed and thus help to support the family.

So my mother worked in Pfizer till she retired at the age of sixty and then was a consultant to the company for a few more years.

She had to go by train to Thane, then take a bus, work hard in the factory, catch a bus to the train station, take a train and then reach home. The work was manual. Technology had not reached Indian shores then.

My dad on the other hand dejectedly entered the workforce. He wanted to work in a bank but for whatever reason that did not happen, and thus he joined Pfizer kicking and screaming. He hated the work. While my mother worked with all her heart and soul, my father worked grudgingly, till he saw my mother and fell in love. He was in love with her till the last moment of his life.

So here you have a woman who wanted only to work, excel, grow and take part in sports, and a man who was least interested in work or sports and was besotted with this beautiful woman.

She had many suitors from the rich and known families of the Zoroastrian community, but she was wanted to focus on her career. She had to help my grandmother and did not want anybody or anything to come in between the well-being of her mother, sisters and brother. My grandfather remained in Hyderabad.

When she was in her mid-twenties, she could no longer bear the pressure from home to get married. One day, tired and frustrated with everything, she announced that she would marry the first man who walked into the house and proposed marriage to her.

Ten minutes later, my dad walked in along with his parents and sought the hand of my exasperated, shell-shocked mother. It was obviously the hand of fate. She thought she recognized my dad and when she came to know that he too worked in Pfizer, she could not overlook the hand of fate and consented.

My mother and father were cheese and chalk. She was a tough woman who could handle any life situation. She did not know the meaning of fear, gave each moment her very best, did not believe in shortcuts, was intelligent, athletic and stood out in the crowd. And then there was my dad. If moodiness was an empire, my dad was its uncrowned emperor. He could bring the house down with his sense of humour and then ten minutes later, he would behave as though he was in intense mourning. He was quick-tempered but calmed down equally fast. He was a child in heart and habit. He worked because he had to work and if there was a shortcut, oh boy, he would take it. He had never played a sport, religiously fell ill and had the least pain threshold ever seen in a man or woman.

But he had the heart of an angel, never held a grudge, helped even those who mistreated or cheated him, was generous to a fault, never wished anybody harm and yes, could never look beyond my mother. Till he lived, my mother got roses, cards on every occasion and birthday gifts; she never had to shop as he would buy every little thing she needed. Often as a kid, he would take me to shops to pick stuff for her, while I pleaded with Baba and Mother Earth to open and consume me.

My mother touched the lives of so many people. Even now people call me up and say they miss my mother. Rich, poor, old, young—she spread her light in all their lives.

She would always tell me that even if an individual has ninety-nine faults and flaws, he/she will have at least one good, redeeming quality in him/her. Always focus on that. Learn how not to behave based on the ninety-nine flaws but do so without judging that individual. Try to emulate that one thing you feel is Godlike or exalting. She lived by that example. She showed me how to treat the saint and sinner with respect and compassion, that we all could slip and make mistakes. We should never let our light and radiance be dulled by entertaining thoughts of darkness and negativity. We all are going to mess up, so do not judge an individual because of one mistake or one character flaw. Go beyond and see the real person. Do not be a fool and trust everybody, but do not be so blinded by life that you doubt everybody.

The second thing she taught me was to give one's heart and soul to all that you do or else to not do that thing at all.

She worked all her life and gave each moment her best. She was promoted and eventually handled the entire medical billing process of Pfizer. She dealt with issues in such a manner that made her colleagues feel safe and secure that she was handling their affairs. I have not met a single individual who did not love her for who she was and the joy and care she brought into their lives. My dad worked all his life in Pfizer only because he could spend time with her. Each morning he would grumble and rant and rave about going to work, but my mom would cajole him and he would oblige like a good boy. There was an inherent sense of dignity about her.

Dad passed away before her and it hit her badly. He was not only her husband but her friend, companion and child too. But she continued working and even three hip surgeries could not stop her.

I have yet to meet anybody as unaffected by money as her. It did not matter to her whether she had money or not. If somebody was in need, she would offer help, without any questions or expectations.

Hours before being operated for a brain tumour, she looked at me and told me two things, 'I have a brain and if I survive but have no memory, take all the decisions and make sure I am consigned to the flames. There are no more vultures left for my body and no matter what pressure is put on you, I do not want chemotherapy. Promise me this.'

The operation was not a success. The cancer had spread extensively and since chemotherapy was ruled out, it was only a matter of months. During that period, she would call me up and talk like a child. I met her two days before she left her body. She wanted to eat ginger biscuits and I managed to get the ones she liked. I fed her a bit and I was told that she did not eat after that. She could not talk much and scribbled on a page that she loved me and that she would see me soon. In spite of all the pain, she sat up and embraced me for one last time.

She passed away an hour or so after midnight. I had just finished my prayers and when the phone rang, I knew my mother was with Baba Sai and Dad. Her ashes, my sister and I scattered in the Arabian Sea. She always wanted to travel. Godspeed Mom.

Be blessed always.

> *My mother taught me a few things with her very presence. She would always tell me that even if an individual has ninety-nine faults and flaws, each individual will have at least one good, redeeming quality in him/her. Always focus on that.*
>
> *We all could slip and make mistakes, so we should never let our light and radiance be dulled by entertaining thoughts of darkness and negativity.*
>
> *She taught me to give one's heart and soul to all that you do or to not do that thing at all.*

20

To Digest or Not

The inability to live a life filled with joy, calmness, peace and without fear of any kind is a state of hell as ruthless as the ones described in the Holy Books.

Look around you and you will realize that people live in a perpetual state of ingratitude. The eternal whiners. Everyone around them is aware how fortunate those idiots are except for these idiots themselves and they continue to whine, never truly removing their heads from their arses.

The Holy Books have various ways of describing hell. The image of hot rods of substandard quality being inserted in the orifices of a poor sod by an overzealous bigot, who is not exceedingly concerned about calories and cholesterol, comes to mind.

When I look around me, I realize that most of us do not know how to digest happiness and peace.

I use the word 'digest' on purpose. My paternal grandad used to tell me often that most people cannot digest a good state of being.

According to Ayurveda, the ancient art of healing using herbs and heaven knows what, it is believed that illness comes forth either from the stomach or the brain.

If one's internal plumbing is not up and running or if one's ability to absorb food calmly is an issue, very soon, in all probability, the other parts of the body will begin to get affected. A clean stomach is a sure sign of good health and a boring diet.

The stomach, according to psychics, is the seat of emotion and if one's emotional state is not good—which means one is married or in love—and is experiencing sensations similar to having one's family jewels nailed to the floor, then the stomach is going to get affected and then the rest is medical history.

So, my grandad would say that most people do not know how to digest happiness and peace. If you give them every reason to be happy, they will create a situation to make themselves unhappy and miserable or ungrateful.

Hence, the inability to digest happiness is a common illness.

Ayurveda states that if the stomach is running like a well-oiled machine, then the cause of illness comes from the head as it is the brain, the seat of consciousness, the seat of not only wants, desires and complexities but also the vehicle that has carried lifetimes of patterns, good, not so good, hilariously horrendous or just the old fashioned—'I came, I saw, I conquered'—kind.

So we have the stomach—with its inability to digest a good thing, and then we have the head—with its the ability to generate greed, hate, lust, and complexities. These are the two seats of illness as well as the two astral bollocks of angst, hate, violence, lust and sadness.

We are becoming a race with playing-the-victim syndrome. It is everybody else's fault but ours. One can have everything and still be miserable. I see it every day. Every time I sit for channelling, it stares me in the face. While someone or the other feels sorry for oneself and plays the victim, a family which has been devastated by death or bankruptcy takes it on the chin calmly. Then there are people who will whine, play the victim or be in a state of ingratitude till I calmly or like a mad man show them the mirror, and if they refuse to see the obvious, I politely tell them to get the fug out.

I see it up close and personal how people want to be in a state of grief and keep playing the victim. The poor-me syndrome. Hell is filled with those playing the victim as living a life of ingratitude and playing the martyr is easier. You refuse to take responsibility for your actions or choices or anything. Rather, you blame, blame and blame everything around you, and if no one is to blame, then God, destiny or fate can always be thrown in. There are so many of us who will crib about the miserable set of cards handed to us by a grumpy God, when in reality we at least have got a set of cards and a pair of hands, something so many people do not get the opportunity to possess . . . and I see this time and again . . . where one chooses darkness over joy, anger over a smile, hate over happy and all I want to say to each one of us is . . . walk away, walk away from false misery and try to do something to help those going through real pain and angst . . . don't become like those people always whining and living in a perpetual state of ingratitude.

Why is our glass always half empty? Why is one's 'calm something' not as good as the neighbour's illusory 'sparkling nothing'? Why does one's loudness in laughter determine one's intensity in happiness? When are we going to truly just be, sigh on seeing the clouds caressing the sky, smell the grass or just take a deep breath . . . when is silence going to be cool, not only outside but within . . . when are we going to tell God, Goddess and Guru, 'Thank You, I am fine. Go and help those truly in need. Come and check on me on and off and sit and gossip with me . . .'

Life is going to kill us. It surely is. When we are gasping for our last few breaths, nothing is going to matter . . . but those moments of joy and happiness we experienced . . . why did we mutilate those beautiful moments with our inane pettiness, jealousy, anger, boorishness or just sheer stupidity?

Why die each day? If there are certain things you can change for the better—change it. If there are things you cannot change—either accept it or move on. We all have a choice. Either to change things or accept them or make a life of hell by neither changing nor accepting nor walking away, but just stewing, hating, creating hell and making life worse.

All are not dictated by the voice of something deep within that forces them to live a life that they do not want to but have to as they have been guided towards it.

Life can finish you off. I have witnessed it at very close quarters through the lives of the innumerable friends who come for guidance.

Destiny, life or fate, for whatever reason, can create hell and make life insufferable. We can't do much at such times except dig our feet and try to go through life calmly and bravely, praying that God, Goddess and Guru gives us the strength and wisdom to go through it with grace and dignity.

Do not create one's own hell and don't make life a living series of misery and grief for oneself and one's loved ones by living in a state of perpetual ingratitude. Remember, there is always somebody living a life more comfortable than ours and millions living lives that make ours seem like a dream. Look around you and you will see true suffering. That doesn't mean our suffering is not real, but we are not alone. Destiny is going to extract its pound of flesh. Even Lord Rama had to go through His suffering along with Maa Sita.

Look at Their lives. Look at the lives of Spiritual Giants and the suffering They underwent. Look at the millions going through poverty, starvation and misery and then try to put your suffering in perspective. Life is going to be as beautiful or beastly as you or I want to make it out to be. Don't let other people's perceptions become your reality and do not let your anger create misery for yourself and those around you.

Just avoid trying to create your own hell.

Learn to digest what life offers you on your platter. Trust me, millions go to sleep on an empty stomach. The only thing they can digest is their state of nothingness.

Be blessed always.

> *When are we going to truly just be, sigh on seeing the clouds caressing the sky, smell the grass or just take a deep breath . . . when is silence going to be cool, not only outside but within?*
>
> *Destiny, life or fate, for whatever reason, can create hell and make life insufferable. We can't do much at such times except dig our feet and try to go through life calmly and bravely, praying that God, Goddess and Guru gives us the strength and wisdom to go through it with grace and dignity.*
>
> *The inability to digest happiness is a common illness.*

21

The Rental

The only certainty about our lives is that one day we are going to drop the body. This fact is the only thing that a sage and a sinner can in harmony agree upon. No matter how one has lived or abused his/her life, the death of our loved ones and eventually one's own self is cast in iron.

But when one looks around or looks within, the way we go about our lives belies this philosophy of mortality. Our very thoughts, words and actions are often on the other side of the mortality barometer. It is as though in flesh we are immortal or worse, we are going to be able to carry with us the fruits of labour, whether ill-gotten or honest, to the other side.

So here is the scenario. We are going to drop the body or die some time in our physical journey and we are not going to carry with us any of the possessions or gains, be it material or that of worldly power, along with us. It does not matter if one is an atheist or believes in life in the spirit world; this reality of passing over without any possessions or power of the physical world is a certainty.

And yet our entire life is spent living as though we are eternal or have some way of taking with us the spoils of our material world.

Yes, I get the need for comfort, security or even luxury. If through hard work one can create a better material life for oneself and our loved ones, it makes perfect sense to strive for such a state of security. Just because one is going to leave the body does not mean one should not live as well as one can.

To pursue one's dreams or fulfil an ambition that one has nurtured since a child gives life a beautiful medley of joy and satisfaction. I get this clearly and am completely in sync with this, but what makes us behave like scheming hyenas? What makes us destroy those who come in our way during our climb to the top? What makes us cheat our loved ones of their rightful inheritance? What makes us try to create a bank balance written with the blood of others? What makes us plot and scheme to get that extra bit which is not needed for survival but makes for just another trophy in one's blood-drenched sack? What makes us behave like animals when we are certain there is no way we can cheat death or be able to take along with us anything apart from the karma we have amassed is something I do not get.

Please, I am part of the whole. I am certain I behave in a similar manner of crass self-destructiveness. But I still don't get it.

When we are sure that we can only take with us our karma and leave behind all else . . . when we are certain that no matter what, only our deeds are going to matter in this long, exhausting marathon . . . yet we behave as though only what is here is real—this astounds me.

Life is a marathon and we still go about it as though it is a hundred-metre dash. We are nuts.

Masters have come and gone, trying to make us see the real picture. This is not it . . . this is just a small sigh in the larger scheme of things . . . this is not permanent . . . this will end . . . but yet we live as though we are immortal and gloat in the glory of our three-dimensional gains.

Where are we going wrong? Does one get obsessively attached to a rental car? So attached that nothing else matters . . . not even one's future? How much ever you have enjoyed travelling in it or driving it, it is a rental and you will have to let go of it . . . you know it, everybody knows it, but you are like a bull on Viagra.

This so-called life or body or material possession is like a rental car. It is important to make sure the car is kept well, taken care of and made as comfortable as possible. But imagine getting obsessed by this rental heap of iron. Killing, cheating, neglecting yourself and your loved ones, your well-being, health and happiness over something that is going to be taken away at some time. The worst part is taking pride in something that is just a rental.

I guess this is what we are doing with our lives, although we know that all this is temporary. The permanent stuff is neglected on a larger level or shoved under the rug. We believe in God, life after death, reincarnation and karma, but we live in a manner that this is it. We know that in the blink of an eye, our destiny can change, but we go about with our eyes shut.

Where a small amount of happiness can be embraced, we wait for a larger piece of the pie. When the larger portion is offered, we want a little more and eventually when that is given, we want it all. We are miserable as we now want a different pie. When we are about to die, moments before the spirit leaves the battered body, I wonder if we are going to remember our bank balance or the position of power or one's looks or strength. I am sure we are going to wonder if there is a life after this body is dropped. If one has lived a life worthy of the next. If the next is going to be miserable due to the ramifications of our free will and the hurt one has caused, and if only there was a little more time, one would have spread more happiness amongst one's lot.

Death is a certainty. There is a section of Buddhists who, every morning after they wake up, lie on the bed, shut their eyes and imagine their own death. They visualize the last moments before the spirit leaves the body. See their loved ones or nobody holding their hands. Those they have loved or fought with are all present, looking down at them, hoping that they overcome death. Then they become a bystander to their own last rites till the body is cremated or buried. Each morning they imagine this whole process of death. The purpose is simple. Witnessing one's death makes one's resolve to live the true life stronger. When you remind yourself each day that someday one is going to pass over, priorities in one's life change for the better. One becomes more compassionate, more liberal, more understanding, more forgiving and large-hearted, and starts using each moment in a far more positive and constructive manner, as who knows, that could well be one's last day.

Sometimes it is important to know how to die, to understand how to live. Death is a transformation. Each day can be used as a means of transformation. If one wears the clock of transformation well, one can exude the fragrance of life in a more humane manner.

There is only one truth about life. It never ends. Change, as Lord Krishna says in the Gita, is the greatest reality. There is permanence only when one merges with The One . . . otherwise, permanence is the greatest myth. There is a saint in every sinner and in every sage there is a sinner waiting to fug up.

The car is rental. Get over it.

Be blessed always.

This so-called life or body or material possession is like a rental car. It is important to make sure the car is kept well, taken care of and made as comfortable as possible. But imagine getting obsessed by this rental heap of iron.

Life is a marathon and we still go about it as though it is a 100-metre dash. We are nuts.

Masters have come and gone, trying to make us see the real picture. This is not it . . . this is just a small sigh in the larger scheme of things . . . this is not permanent . . . this will end . . . but yet we live as though we are immortal and gloat in the glory of our three-dimensional gains.

Sometimes it is important to know how to die, to understand how to live. Death is a transformation. Each day can be used as a means of transformation. If one wears the clock of transformation well, one can exude the fragrance of life in a more humane manner.

22

On the Wings of Forgiveness

According to me, all spirituality stems forth from one's belief that the individual is the energy, the spark and the sigh of the Creator. Thus in reality, each one of us embodies divinity in varying degrees.

So it all begins with the realization or conviction of one being the Spirit Energy rather than matter; the former embodies eternalness, while the latter is a mirage of permanence.

The second important realization comes forth from the firm belief that God is just and noble and thus cannot be partial or unfair.

Thus, God exists and He does not take sides and to make certain no sides are taken, He does not intervene in either the process or the ramifications of one's thoughts, words and deeds.

If you believe in God, then inevitably the concept of karma follows.

What is karma? As you sow, so shall you reap. Sow weed and you are going to get a beautiful yield of . . . weed. All that we reap is the result of what we have sown. God has got nothing to do with the sowing or the reaping. He/She watches aghast as we go about cutting our own feet with supreme daftness.

Thus, all that we experience in the form of discomfort or calmness, grief or joy, wealth of various kinds or poverty of all kinds, is the harvest we reap. Yes, karma and the future are fluid, dependent on the use of whatever free will one has left in the terribly depleted spiritual reservoir. It is a complicated business and many times we just want to finish with the stinking mire of give and take and the karmic web, so we try to take on as much as possible.

If everything is either about attaining rewards or cleansing and balancing, then in reality the concept of repentance and seeking absolution should take centre stage.

It is actually simple. The ill-advised use of free will leads to having one's nose rubbed into hard and thorny grounds as well as some dork nailing the family jewels to the floor. It is exceedingly painful and terribly humbling. I would have used more poetic and appropriate words to describe the process but then each one of us has already gone through this mind-numbing process, so why rub salt to the battered body?

We pay for our actions that have caused others pain. I mean I can't think of anything more damning than to cause pain to others or oneself.

Yes, I am sure there must be other ways of truly messing up one's karmic balance sheet, but I do not think anything can get one's scale heavier than hurting others. The intensity may range from mild to severe, but more than often we are being cleansed, thrashed, mauled and having our sanity clinically amputated due to the pain, grief, hurt and heartache we have caused others, through lifetimes of self-centredness, weakness and stupidity.

We all call ourselves spiritual, but when going through our own hell, how many times do we wonder what wrong we must have done and to whom, to go through such harrowing grief and pain? If I am suffering and God exists—and God is just—I am being cleansed of all the karmic sludge which I have carried with me; most of it must have come from hurting others. If I were to believe in the laws of karma—which is the very foundation of eternal life—and if somebody breaks my heart or deceives me, if justice has been denied to me, if my children are taken away, if I have been manipulated and if I have been wronged, then I must have broken hearts, deceived, floundered and manipulated others in the past.

Our karmic debt can only be this heavy if we have messed up this bad. Why else would one have his/her heart yanked out metaphorically, in spite of the individual? I have begun thinking of all this and very often, subconsciously, my heart goes out to all those whom I have hurt, knowingly or unknowingly; those I have caused pain; those whom I have deceived; those whose trust I have broken and caused heartbreak . . . I am ashamed . . . not wiser, just ashamed . . . and I have begun to seek their forgiveness.

Now I know the confession box or booth is as therapeutic to the earnest as it is to the hypocrite. But if an individual is truly in the heart-wringing process of repentance, then I believe the prayer of forgiveness can release one from the bonds of hurt, pain and hate that one shares with others, carried forward from and for lifetimes.

This is how I think it works. First we have to understand that we all have obviously messed up, often through the journeys where we walked about in self-centred smog. Now, we have hurt others. Yes, others have hurt us too. We have wronged and been wronged. We have deceived and been deceived. But where does all this end? I hurt you. You hurt me in some other lifetime. Maybe you have hurt me a little more and so now I seek justice. In the next lifetime, I want to dish out whatever justice the books of accounts can hand over to me. So I again hurt you . . .

the laws of karma state that there should be no accounts left . . . but so often, there are accounts remaining to be paid . . . they are carried forward to the next lifetime . . . and this crippling dance of hate continues.

What if one wants to step out from this dance? We do not know how many accounts are floating about waiting to smack us in the face. The concept of repentance and seeking forgiveness becomes truly important in such a scenario.

When you in earnest begin to feel horrible with just the notion of having hurt, deceived and troubled others; of having been slanderous and bad-mouthed; of having spread malicious lies and gossip; of breaking hearts and trusts in this lifetime or another, one begins to bleed from within and the first step towards freeing yourself from this web of hate commences.

The bleeding is good. Bad blood has to be drained out of one's being. The dirty water has to be removed from the vessel and the vessel has to be cleaned. One can then use the vessel to fill fresh water to quench one's thirst. This cleansing can begin only through repentance and by seeking forgiveness.

What does this process of repentance and yearning for mercy truly achieve? Well, first and foremost, it makes one realize what a stupid worm one has been, thus triggering this strange alien emotion called humility, which slowly but surely seems to have gone out of circulation. True humility comes from knowing we all are the same, in varied hues of spiritual evolvement or degradation.

When one repents and seeks pardon for one's sins of omission and commission, and truly means and feels it, one is operating from compassion and selflessness. This comes forth from the higher self. Just as it has come from our higher self, our true repentance reaches the higher self of all those who we have hurt. Vibrations attract. All those we are entwined with through the bonds of karma are connected through our auras too. Like a complex electrical power box, there are so many wires—each one oblivious that they are linked to each other, but working in unison, in the circumference of their usage or destiny.

Our higher selves seek forgiveness and the vibrations of forgiveness—a cry of repentance—is sent out to the cosmos. It reaches all those antennas connected to one's karmic satellite and one's plea of mercy is felt, heard and slowly acknowledged by the higher self of those we have done wrong. Slowly, the bond of hate, negativity, anger and the need to seek revenge and justice starts to diminish and a new bond of compassion is formed.

I have seen it work with many people; numerous folks have come back to narrate strange stories of reconciliation and calmness with those who were once a source of serious discomfort, indigestion and ulcers.

But you truly need to mean it and feel it. It is not just an exercise to worm one's way out of a difficult situation.

One's prayers are heard and so is the sigh of repentance and seeking forgiveness.

So you have the higher selves going about with their song and dance. I also believe that one's intentions touch a chord with the Archangels, spirit workers or light warriors, guides and guardian Angels, who then intervene and sort of knock sense into the higher self of others or into the lower self of the dork crying about for blood, justice and revenge.

I also believe that the ancestors of those who have been wronged, sensing the intention of the one praying for pardon, too play a role. They might realize the honesty of the prayer and begin to work their magic on the situation. Blessing is a truly powerful tool to spread peace and compassion. Who knows, if the ancestors are convinced, they might even intervene and ease the situation currently stuck in the abyss of hate and revenge.

The most important benefit of repentance and the act of seeking forgiveness is that it makes the individual more compassionate and most importantly, more forgiving in his/her attitude and behaviour towards others. How funny would it be if I pray and go on about seeking forgiveness and in the very next breath, I want revenge and someone's pound of flesh? It could only mean I am not truly repentant or I am a classified nutjob.

When one prays for forgiveness, one acknowledges one's own fragility and that one has feet of clay too. It does wonders to deflate the ego and also creates calmness within to deal with the idiosyncrasies of others. There is so much to seek forgiveness for from God, Goddess and Guru too. No wonder then that in the *Avesta*, the Zoroastrian religious texts, the prayer of repentance goes on and on. The translation of the prayer makes you realize how many times in a day we must have saddened one's God, Goddess and Guru; it breaks one's heart and makes one want to dig a hole and crawl into it.

Crying out for mercy is an act of repentance and shows the desire to start afresh with all those one has been hurtful towards. We mess up countless times each day. So it would be advisable to first seek forgiveness from one's God, Goddess and Guru, as through our thoughts, words and deeds, we truly hurt The One and also many others, knowingly or otherwise.

The need to seek forgiveness and repent is also the first step of one's own healing process. It is an acknowledgment to The One that you have messed up. This has nothing to do with lessening the intensity of the karmic cleansing, but simply that 'I am ashamed for having caused suffering to others. Lord, please forgive me for I have sinned and done wrong to others. I am truly sorry for all those who I have hurt in any manner.'

Seeking mercy from The One leads one to seek forgiveness from all those we have hurt in this lifetime or in the past. It makes one cautious about not adding more weight to the cross one carries of hurt, anger, revenge and hate.

So, one seeks forgiveness from all those who one has hurt and one seeks to forgive all those bastards who have hurt us . . .

just kidding . . . and one seeks forgiveness from God, Goddess and Guru.

And then the final sigh . . . one begins to seek forgiveness from oneself too for behaving in such a manner and causing pain to others, and thus causing pain to oneself in the form of karmic burden to trudge along for lifetimes.

I truly believe this is something we need to do and I also know that this can work wonders on various levels, but most importantly, it is the first step towards walking back to our Real Home.

Be blessed always.

Prayer of forgiveness from Baba Sai of Shirdi through channelling:

My God, Goddess, Guru,

I first and foremost seek Your forgiveness for ever hurting You or showing my back to Your Radiance and Love. Forgive me, forgive me, forgive me.

Have mercy on me and my loved ones. Treat me and my loved ones gently, though I have sinned through my thoughts, words, intent and actions.

I know I have blundered but I am Yours and thus I plead with Thou to treat me and my loved ones with tenderness and mercy. I do not deserve Your love or Your compassion, but I pray for Your love and mercy.

I also seek forgiveness for all thoughts, words, intent and actions that have caused hurt and pain to any being in this lifetime or in any other, ever.

I repent for my sins done knowingly or unknowingly and thus hurting anybody known (the name of the individual) or not known. I truly seek forgiveness from all. Truly forgive me.

I seek pardon from those I have deceived, and from their loved ones and ancestors too.

If in any way I have caused anybody ruin, I truly seek forgiveness and repent my thoughts, words, intent and deeds that caused it.

I pray that the bond of hurt, hate, revenge, anger, violence, malice and slander be removed and a bond of love, peace and compassion prevail.

So be it as I pray, so be it as I plead, so be it as I seek pardon. Amen.

True humility comes from knowing we all are the same, in varied hues of spiritual evolvement or degradation.

When one repents and seeks pardon for one's sins of omission and commission, and truly means and feels it, one is operating from compassion and selflessness. This comes forth from the higher self. All those we are entwined with through the bonds of karma are connected through our auras too. Like a complex electrical power box, there are so many wires——each one oblivious that they are linked to each other, but working in unison, in the circumference of their usage or destiny.

One's prayers are heard and so is the sigh of repentance and seeking forgiveness.

The most important miracle of repentance is that it makes the individual more compassionate and most importantly, more forgiving in his/her attitude and behaviour towards others.

When one prays for forgiveness, one acknowledges one's own fragility and that one has feet of clay. It does wonders to deflate the ego and also creates calmness within to deal with the idiosyncrasies of others.

23

The Halo of Fear

Very often people want to know how they can make their lives more spiritual. They are tired of the constant badgering going on in their heart and mind. Fears of various kinds plague their souls. They are aware that this is not the life they want to lead but more often than not, they come to the conclusion that there is no light at the end of the tunnel. To see light at the end of the tunnel, they must come to the end of the passageway, and this burrow through which they traverse—the tunnel of the mind—has no ending. It is virtually infinite. Thus to expect to see any sort of hope or glimmer of light of any kind is out of the question.

We are a society living in the abyss of our fears. We have so many fears that to distract ourselves from the darkness, we do not mind playing with any sort of glitter. The fact is life is as simple as we want it to be or as macabre as we make it to be.

We are a species obsessed with uncertainties and paranoia. Most often, the very foundations of our relationships are based not on love but insecurities, ego, societal pressures and a misguided sense of the much-abused, four-letter word . . . love.

153

We have not even left God in our psychotic scheme of things.

Look around us and we will realize that if fear was not so rampant, may be God would be remembered the way we remember our ancestors, once a year, for an hour or so.

The greatest tragedy is that most of us pray or look towards God because we are scared of something going wrong or to seek something for ourselves or our loved ones. Do we pray because we love God or because we are scared or simply self-centred? When was the last time we knelt in prayer because we truly and genuinely felt selfless love for our God, Goddess and Guru? I mean, when was the last time we prayed because we felt true love for The One? I can remember countless times when I prayed to Baba Sai because I feared something or needed something . . . but when was the last time I truly prayed to Him, out of love? Even thanking Him could have been to appease Him through a self-centred sense of gratitude, so that the bounty keeps coming forth, but when was it that I prayed to Him because I truly love Him, miss Him and want to share my love for Him with Him? I can't remember.

I know we pray because we are so tired of being dictated by karmic retribution, which comes forth from our imbecility or greed from other lifetimes or in my case, from this lifetime. Every time something is going wrong in my life, I seem to pray harder and for a longer time. Such prayer does not come forth from love; it comes forth from fear, as a plea to be saved.

When was the last time I prayed to You, my Old Man, out of sheer love? I can't remember, Baba.

We chant mantras or go through elaborate rituals of prayers, which later becomes a rite one has to go through, in the hope of appeasing one's God, Goddess and Guru, one of the nine planets or some megalomaniac ancestor. Love or gratitude of the selfless kind is long buried under the debris of ritualism or sheer business.

Our faith is thus dictated by our fear. Sometimes I think that the greater our fear, the more intense is our prayer. In fact, so often, even our very goodness comes forth from the fear of retribution or in the hope of pleasing The One, so that the bounties of indulging in good thoughts, good words and good deeds are showered upon us.

Are we truly noble or is nobility a cloak we wear because we have sort of comprehended the workings of karma and realized that 'as you sow, you daft gnome, so shall you reap'? Am I noble because of the need for nobility or am I walking the path only because I am aware where the other paths lead to and don't want to go that way?

I have known many who have clearly told me that they are plodding along the by-lanes of Light and spirituality because they were trounced by either destiny or a demonic or ruthless individual. They had nowhere to go to seek refuge but to their God, Goddess and Guru, and thus their dwelling in and traversing the path of Light is the result of their circumstance or an individual.

Most of us have enjoyed the beautiful fragrance of the earth because we have got our noses rubbed into the ground. Otherwise we would have continued our journey, with our fat heads way up in the clouds.

Thus, most often, our spirituality is the result of our fears. The shimmering aura around our head is the halo of fear. However, this does not apply to everybody. I am sure there are many who are spiritual because they love The One and all that. Good for you.

When people ask how to make life more spiritual or simple, what they really want to know is how to go beyond the complexities of fear.

We all are in the same boat, but on different seats.

I think all spirituality, even if the reasons may be that of fear or escapism, should eventually lead to the path of genuine love and selfless gratitude to the Big Boy. I don't want my child to keep repeating my name or how good I am or how generous I am or how merciful I am. I want my child to just love me. I guess this goes for The One too. That is the only way forward.

If I am good, noble or spiritual for any other reason but true love for the God, Goddess and Guru, then I am entering into a commercial arrangement with The One. As I have written earlier, God is a lousy businessman. The chap doesn't understand anything of profit and loss or debit and credit. He/She is positively bordering on dyslexia and is numerically challenged. Avoid business transactions at all cost. You are going to incur serious loss along with maleficent ulcers.

Spirituality has become a business now. The trump card is that of fear. Don't play the game. The deck is for sure held against us. The only reason we should be playing the game is because we love the game and love to play it with the Boss.

I guess when we understand that true love has no place for fear, there is less likelihood of us being hoodwinked into a life that our true self does not identify with. We should be spiritual because we love The One. We should spend time in doing good stuff and pray because all this spiritual *naach gaana* makes you and me feel more connected with the Old Geezer. Both the spiritual path and prayer should have its foundations only in true love and gratitude. With true love and selfless gratitude comes the need to seek forgiveness. When you love, you begin to realize the pain caused to the lover, and the need to seek pardon for that pain will gush forth from the deepest recess of the heart and soul.

When one prays or walks the path out of compulsion, of either circumstances or fear, the divine fragrance and radiance make their presence felt through their sheer absence.

Life is beautifully complicated and then when we throw in the baggage of one's upbringing and add to it the weight of the karmic cross, things are only going to get more interesting, to say the least. At such times, compassion towards yourself, your circumstances, those around you, the dorks who are making life miserable, destiny, the planets and the drunk spirit chaps manning the spirit dimensions is going to make the journey a little less stressful and complicated as well as less mind-numbing.

True compassion comes forth from love. When you are in love with God, Goddess and Guru, and all you want is to make Him/Her happy and proud of you, not for anything else, but because you love the Old Goat, then life begins to get simpler, spirituality less complicated and more selfless. Also you begin to get less judgemental and that makes a huge difference in your flight towards The One.

Remember that both the darkness and the rainbow are a play of light. Just enjoy the psychotic show.

Be blessed always.

The fact is life is as simple as we want it to be or as macabre as we make it to be.

When people ask how to make life more spiritual or simple, what they really want to know is how to go beyond the complexities of fear.

When we understand that true love has no place for fear, there is less likelihood of us being hoodwinked into a life that our true self does not identify with.

Both the spiritual path and prayer should have its foundations only in true love and gratitude. With true love and selfless gratitude comes the need to seek forgiveness. When you love, you begin to realize the pain caused to the lover, and the need to seek pardon for that pain will gush forth from the deepest recess of the heart and soul.

When one prays or walks the path out of a compulsion, of either circumstances or fear, the divine fragrance and radiance make their presence felt through their sheer absence.

Remember that both the darkness and the rainbow are a play of light.

24

God Isn't Deaf, We Are Mute

Praying to one's God, Goddess and Guru is one of the most personal interactions between an individual and the one he/she believes in. There is no set method or formula on how one should communicate with the powers beyond and within.

Of course, each religion and religious texts prescribe certain ways or the methodology of how one needs to pray. The manner in which one needs to prepare for prayer so often varies according to religion. Yes, each one advocates that the body needs to be cleaned. A bath would be ideal. I guess God likes the fragrance of soap and powder. Then one needs to wear clean clothes.

There is a prescribed direction one has to face while praying. Zoroastrians are usually told to face the sun and if, for whatever reason, that is not possible, then one is told to face the south as according to me, when one faces the south, one's back is never to the sun. For Zoroastrians, facing the north is clearly not advised but in *vaastu* and according to various prayers said to Lord Shiva and Goddess Kali, it is advocated. The Muslims are told to face the holy Kaaba. So in India, a Muslim would face the West, but if he/she is in another continent, the person would face say, the north, south or east.

Some religions prescribe headgear too. Headgear is mandatory for Zoroastrians, Muslims, Sikhs and Jews, while it is not required for Hindus, Buddhists, Jains and Christians.

Zoroastrians, Jews, Christians and Muslims never pray bare feet. There has to be a prayer mat, a rug, a sheet of cloth, socks, slippers or even shoes. That would be seen as a sign of great disrespect where Hindus, Sikhs, Buddhists and Jains are concerned.

Some religions consider it a sin for women to enter the place of worship while she is menstruating. Hindus and Zoroastrians consider it blasphemy, while Christians and Sikhs do not seem to have any issue with it.

As a Zoroastrian, I know for a fact that it does not matter what food one has consumed before entering a Fire Temple. But it would be sacrilege for many Hindus to learn of somebody consuming meat and visiting a temple. First pay your respect to God, Goddess and Guru and then stuff your face with whatever you so desire.

Thus, there are many ways of praying that Holy Books advocate, some even contradictory to each other.

I am sure there are good reasons for every such prescribed religious modus operandi, custom and tradition. I would have written about all that but then like always, I am clueless.

Just as each religious tradition advocates a particular diet for one's spiritual growth, so is the case with the method of prayers. I have mentioned this before: if diet was so important for spiritual growth and if each religious custom, spoken or assumed, is writ in stone, then there would have to be various heavens based on each one's diet.

For a Jain, even consuming an onion hinders spiritual growth. A Muslim abstains from eating pork while a Hindu worships the cow, but may eat chicken, fish, eggs and pork. A Zoroastrian and a Christian will consume any blasted thing leisurely walking, swimming or flying about. So, either there is one heaven that goes beyond diet or there are various heavens depending on what one has stuffed his/her face with while on earth.

Thus, there are various ways to pray and eat that pleases the Lord. So says the religious texts or the interpretations of the religious texts.

So how does one pray? Does one cover the head or not? Wear shoes or stand bare feet? Loudly or softly? After bath or before? What if you want to pray when there is no water or you can't go and freshen up? What if one doesn't have a fresh set of clothes? What if a chap cleaning the sewer wants to reach out to his/her God, Goddess and Guru while his/her feet are deep in shit and piss and their clothes and body are stinking? Yes, the head is covered but there is dirt floating about. He/she is deep down in the sewage pit, the sun is not visible and hence the direction is unknown. What if the person suddenly wants to pray in such a situation? What then? Does his/her prayer not reach God, Goddess and Guru? Does He/She suffer from an obsessive compulsive disorder for cleanliness? A fetish for cologne and moisturizer? I hope not. For God's sake, I hope not.

So the question is, if a person who is working in a sewer can pray and his/her prayer's reach The One, then obviously there is something that the individual is doing right, apart from not concentrating on his/her work.

Despite going against everything prescribed by those who claim to interpret the words of the Prophet, The One seems to have heard the prayer of the individual.

What does that mean? I know for certainty that you can scrub the skin off your arse with the most expensive body wash, wear clothes made out of the finest cloth and follow every rule prescribed in the Holy Book, but if your heart and soul and your love is not in prayer, I truly have my doubts if your prayers are going to pass through the depleted ozone layer and the smog of pollution encasing our planet. There needs to be power for anything to defy gravity and our prayers, if not fuelled by pure, innocent love, gratitude and yearning, will not have the velocity to break through and go beyond the beyond. We hardly get our network connection on our mobile phones when we are in a lift, so imagine how difficult it would be to connect to the Boss who has a very questionable network system.

It would be safe to deduce that the power of prayer is more in the heart and spirit, and in the love and yearning for the Elusive One, rather than the attire, sense of hygiene and modus operandi. Yes, it would be great if you were to follow whatever is told to you by your elders, but that is just packaging. We know by now that, most often, packaging is a surreal way of fooling everybody, including oneself, about the true contents within.

For me, the best way to pray is when you truly send yourself to The One, or pull Him/Her to come and sit in front of you. Either your love and thoughts travel to The One, where you can see Him/Her or the energy in your mind's eye, or you can feel Him/Her or the energy sitting or standing a few feet away from you, hearing you, sensing your love and feeling your yearning. He/She may be bored listening to the drivel being dished out, but *kya kare,* there is no option as your prayer, like a magnet, pulls the Chap closer and closer.

Imagine you are praying with such love that you are certain that whatever your God, Goddess and Guru is doing, He/She will leave everything and hear you pray for those seconds, moments or minutes—will feel your prayers and your love. Imagine and believe that if you pray with true love, the Old Drifter will stop gallivanting, halt and hear you out. He/She has no option. He/She is our parent. No parent will ever neglect the true pleading or craving of one's child. It is not possible that if our child reaches out to us with true love, we will not leave everything to just listen and be there. Why would God, Goddess and Guru be any different? They are our universal parents, mother, father, brother, sister, friend, grandparents, counsellor and quacks, all rolled into one. So according to me, and I could be completely wrong, if we were to pray in this manner, They will halt and listen.

Or pray in such a way that The One is pulled towards you, into your room where you are praying, and is made to sit right in front of you. Hearing us pray, communicate or speak some heartfelt poppycock. How would we pray if Sai Baba of Shirdi or one's God, Goddess and Guru actually materialized in front of us and looked on as we prayed? I am certain our entire approach to prayer would be different. We would completely be there. Present in body, mind, heart and soul. We would forget everything and everybody, and all the inane stuff we stuff our beings with, and just be. We would pray with an intensity which one would think is not possible.

It doesn't matter what we wear, where we are, if we have shoes on or not, if we have headgear or not, if we have taken a bath or not—nothing in reality can stand a chance to one's love and dedication.

As we pray, we start interacting with The One, as He/She truly is, beyond form, just energy and spirit. And as we are from The One, we too are just energy and spirit in our true essence. Imagine oneself to be just energy or spirit, without the body. As we drop the body, our God, Goddess and Guru will drop His/Her body too and then no formality of prayers will matter, as in the world of spirit, the only thing that matters is pure love and intention.

As we see ourselves as energy and the Top Boss we pray to as pure energy, a time will come when we metamorphose into calmer beings from disgruntled dorks. We become a pure spirit and may in our imagination or reality merge with The One, who is energy personified.

Prayer is a private dance you have with The One. You choose your set-up, attire, rhythm, tune, lyrics and most importantly, your pace and create your own dance. Hold the Chap close to you, making sure the Blighter holds you close too.

Every time you chant His/Her name, even if it is for those micro seconds, forget everything but The One. Believe that as you call out with complete devotion and love, He/She will leave all and listen to you with complete devotion and love or come and be in front of you, as God is a sucker for pure love.

God has existed much before we came into the picture and messed up things. God will remain much after we have been sort of deleted from the main frame. But trust me, even God will miss those private conversations, the love, the yearning and the madness. Sometimes I feel it is those moments of love that forces The One to let this circus of life continue.

God isn't deaf. If we truly pray with our heart, then He/She begins to hear our words. Otherwise, our voice doesn't defy gravity. There is nothing noisier than a preoccupied mind; I doubt if He/She cares too much for the mutterings of a distracted heart.

Be blessed always.

The power of prayer is more in the heart and spirit, and in the love and yearning for the Elusive One, rather than in the attire, sense of hygiene and modus operandi.

For me, the best way to pray is to truly send yourself to The One or pull Him/Her to come and sit in front of you. Either your love and thoughts travel to The One, where you can see Him/Her or the energy in your mind's eye, or you can feel Him/Her or the energy sitting or standing a few feet away from you, hearing you, sensing your love and feeling your yearning.

Imagine you are praying with such love that you are certain that whatever your God, Goddess and Guru is doing, He/She will leave everything and hear you pray for those seconds, moments or minutes—will feel your prayers and your love.

Prayer is a private dance you have with The One. You choose your set-up, attire, rhythm, tune, lyrics and most importantly, your pace and create your own dance. Hold the Chap close to you, making sure the Blighter holds you close too.

As we pray, we start interacting with The One, as He/She truly is, beyond form, just energy and spirit.

25

Happiness and All That . . .

Whenever we are asked what we truly desire or pray for, we usually declare that we are looking for happiness and peace.

The problem is both happiness and peace are non-tangible, evasive chaps.

What is happiness and peace of mind in reality? Very often, when I look back to my battered past, I have realized that I have been in a state of happiness and peace, but most of the times never even appreciated that state till something or the other put me in a state of unhappiness and unrest.

Does one have to be in a state of conflict and unease to value contentment and peace of mind? Quite often, there is nothing happening and one goes about one's day in a capsule of normalcy. Unless fate is a truly exasperating one, normalcy usually is a safe womb of nothingness. I equate those times of normalcy to peace and happiness, which can eventually only come about when you nurture that state of quietude and calmness.

I nowadays pray for an uneventful day. It is a safe zone to be in. Uneventful means that external conflict and unease are kept at bay.

If all is quiet on the external front, there is no true reason to be at unease internally and that is a good enough state of serenity to be in.

Writing this garbled outpouring, I sit on the balcony, watching the sky. It has rained somewhere. Patches of the sky are pregnant with grey clouds which seem to be moving about without any hurry or mission. The sun is trying its best to peek through, colouring the sky behind the clouds gold. There is breeze in the air. The house resounds with the soft caress of chants. There are two crows that seem to have a lot to talk about. One of them obviously has difficulty in hearing, thus the loud conversation. I can see kids playing in the garden and now can partially see the sun. It is truly beautiful. I am in a state of stillness. I doubt if anything can surpass this state of calm nothingness. Because I took the time to see the sky, the crazy crows, the peeking sun, the movement of the clouds, I have, maybe for a few minutes, found my state of tranquillity and thus found my peace. I am certain this state of serenity will not last for long, but that is fine as may be the greater the state of unease, the stronger the possibility of one enjoying tender moments just to be in harmony with oneself and everything around and within me.

Who knows, maybe when I am about to leave the body, it is these moments that might flash in front of me, making the entire act of passing over serene.

Happiness is a state of mind. What can give us happiness now may be a cause of discomfort later on. And vice versa. Peace is a state of being. You can insist on being in a state of calm stillness and make it a priority and who knows, through most of the day, a certain sense of calmness may pervade you, even though nothing extraordinary might be taking place . . . or in our words . . . there is no logical reason to be happy.

I have realized, though I fail embarrassedly too often in the day, that when one makes peace of mind and a state of calmness one's priority, one usually finds ways of holding on to serenity for a longer period of time. How much do you and I want peace? How desperately do we want a state of calmness? If there is an urgency for peace and calmness, we will enter the arena of conflict or reaction with less frequency.

The first thing that will happen is that our reactions will reduce, as nothing creates disharmony within and outside as the propensity to react—silently, voraciously or violently.

The crows seem to be having a board meeting. Now two more have come and the chaps are stone deaf. Anyway, where was I? Yes, when we stop reacting, we start being more open and compassionate. I feel most of our issues are due to our tendency of reacting to everything.

Usually, a bout requires two boxers in the ring. If you walk away, sit back and calmly talk, at least from your side, the ability to hold on to one's centredness is greater. If peace of mind is one's priority and that brings about a state of relative happiness, then the more distance we keep between reactions, the greater the chance of enjoying a state of stillness.

One can start their day by offering a necklace of calmness to one's God, Goddess and Guru and most importantly, to oneself. Each pearl in the necklace can signify a moment of harmony. I understand clearly that there will be moments and days when one will feel crushed by the weight of circumstances, adversity, desperation and depression, but I can only hope and pray that those days are spaced far in between. But even here, if one perseveres for calmness and peace, the crushing burden will be marginally easier to bear.

The more often one can be in a state of calmness, the more ingrained is the level of serenity. Eventually, one is embraced with a sense of silent happiness.

Seeking any gratification for the soul and spirit from anything external is like expecting to convincingly explain the colours of the rainbow to someone who has not seen it.

External stuff will give gratification to only that part of us which is made up of the five elements. If one is fixated on the external, then yes, external gratification, for a while, appeases one's senses connected to the flesh. Nothing wrong with it. But if one is truly talking of happiness and peace, then one needs to be in a state of harmony within, than what the credit card can bring home.

Now the crows have flown off to wherever crows go at night. It is twilight now. A plane passes through the dark clouds. Two clouds are in the process of embracing each other, making the patch of blue sky slowly disappear. That moment of sheer bliss has passed. But the memory of it shall linger for a long time. I am sure for whatever little time it cocooned me in her warm embrace, it must have done something to enhance my overall well-being, body, heart, mind and soul.

Life will move on. Our loved ones will leave us or we will leave them. There will be strife. Unrest. Agitation. Tears. Heartbreak. Ill health. The graph of life will have its peaks and lows. The important thing is to remain still within. Grasp the little moments that calm us. God, Goddess, Guru and all calmness lie within. What matters is how passionately one wants to hold on to Them.

Lord Krishna has said, 'Those who remember Me at the time of death will come to Me. Do not doubt this. Whatever occupies the mind at the time of death determines the destination of the dying; they will always tend towards that state of being.'

The fact is that our body is preparing for our death each moment. We are moving towards the final goodbye where our spirit shall be yanked out of our bodies. This journey has begun from the moment we were born and occupied a body.

Did Lord Krishna only refer to the final crossover? Or did He mean to think of Him, God, Goddess and Guru at every moment, as our body, breath and cells are dying every moment. Even if He did mean the final separation of the spirit from the body and to be in the moment of pure oneness with Krishna or one's God, Goddess and Guru, one needs to bring forth the consciousness of living in a state of stillness and peace or calm acceptance and surrender within. One needs to know how to hold on to Him/Her when the final good riddance comes forth.

We have got a lot of stuff wrong. At least I have. But I do pray that you and me begin to nurture short embraces of stillness so that when the time truly comes for us to get wings, we are already living in brief states of Oneness, calmness, harmony or whatever name one wants to give the state of being.

Be blessed always.

> *When one makes peace of mind and a state of calmness one's priority, one usually finds ways of holding on to serenity for a longer period of time.*
>
> *If peace of mind is one's priority and that brings about a state of relative happiness, then the more distance we keep between reactions, the greater the chance of enjoying a state of stillness.*
>
> *One can start each day by offering a necklace of calmness to one's God, Goddess and Guru and most importantly, to oneself. Each pearl in the necklace can signify a moment of harmony.*
>
> *Seeking any gratification for the soul and spirit from anything external is like expecting to convincingly explain the colours of the rainbow to someone who has not seen it.*
>
> *God, Goddess, Guru and all calmness lie within. What matters is how passionately one wants to hold on to Them.*

26

The Quest for a Master

Do we choose our Master or does our Master choose us?

If you want me to sound esoteric, I will tell you, 'No, we don't choose our Master, our Master chooses us.'

To a very large extent it is true because *apni aukaat kahaan hai* (we don't have the potential) to choose a Master. He/She decides.

But this association with the Master has been going on for lifetimes. It's not as though the Guru standing on the road says, 'He/she really wants me. Let Me make a disciple out of the idiot.'

There is nothing random at play here.

Eventually, we have to go back to our past lives, to the association between us and our Masters.

At that particular point, maybe He/She wasn't a Spiritual Master, but a normal human being working his/her way through the karmic mire. But nonetheless, there has to be some karmic association which has come to fructify in this present day and time. Now that same individual, through discipline and selfless love for The One and one and all, has evolved as a Master, but your association exists in the by-lanes of the past.

Does the Master choose you? Honestly, no. Eventually, one's karma chooses the relationship between the Master and the disciple.

There has to be some foundation for this relationship. It could be that of a mother and a child; the child has lost his/her way whereas the mother has grown internally and progressed to becoming a Spiritual Master and then, may be after eighty-four births, a Perfect Master.

The fact remains that a mother will never forget her child; neither will the Master forget His/Her own.

So when the mother's energy has metamorphosed into that of a Perfect Master, the Master, who has also traversed various lifetimes, will start searching for all of His/Her associations . . . and create circumstances where the child and the mother meet.

But the foundation has been laid down by both the Master and the disciple, maybe before innumerable lifetimes. The groundwork was cemented and this lifetime just becomes the culmination.

There are no coincidences. There has to be some karma involved.

Why is it that some people have so much of love for one Master and when they look at another Master, they feel nothing at all? It does not mean that they are lacking in devotion or there is something amiss in the Master. It just means they don't have a karmic bond that goes back lifetimes and thus there is no internal connect. No intermingling of auras.

My bond with Baba must have formed lifetimes before because in this lifetime, I have done nothing to deserve either being a channel or His love.

So, it is His grace that has led to this union; it has got to do with something in our past. I must have done something to tickle His funny bone and forced Him to say, 'The boy is an idiot but he is Mine.'

Thus, I believe this holiest of unions, between a Master and the disciple, is karmic. What these fancy guys call *Ranubhandha* . . . karmic bond, and it is through this bond that everything comes about.

It is difficult to say who chooses whom. But yes, the Master finds His/Her own and brings them all home.

Jai Baba.

Be blessed always.

> *Eventually, one's karma chooses the relationship between the Master and the disciple.*
>
> *The fact remains that a mother will never forget her child, neither will the Master forget His/Her own.*
>
> *I believe this holiest of unions, between a Master and the disciple, is karmic. What these fancy guys call Ranubhandha . . . the karmic bond . . . it is through this bond that everything comes about.*
>
> *When the mother's energy has metamorphosed into that of a Perfect Master, the Master, who has also traversed various lifetimes, will start searching for all of His/Her associations . . . and create circumstances where the child and the mother meet.*

27

My Dearest Baba Sai

Dearest Baba Sai. I know You must be truly busy. You have scores of devotees. Millions upon millions of people who love You. I am not going to get into true love, self-centred love or need-based love . . . whatever form of love, we all love You. What makes one believe that his/her love is purer or truer or more divine than another lover of Yours. As a parent, You know each child and their potential, goodness, stupidity and priorities, but where love is concerned, You are so tender and merciful that Your love is for all . . . a parent loves each child, whether he/she deserves it or not.

I know that every single child of Yours shares a beautiful personal bond with You, so very different from the other. From the big life-altering stuff or disillusionments to the most trivial and inane prattle, each one must, I am sure, reveal all to You and go through each experience with You and then either praise You, blame You or defend You.

I know Baba that You are busy. I do not know how You do this. How do You somehow manage to be with each one of us? You are truly present, in spite of us being so truly closed up, full of mental-emotional-karmic baggage. You know what Baba Sai, I do not comprehend how You do this, each moment of each second of each minute of each hour of each day of each week of each month of each year of each lifetime, every lifetime, lifetime after lifetime, beyond this plane and in all the worlds. Maybe I will understand how You do it but I will never comprehend why You do it.

Why do You keep working on us and believing in our inherent goodness and trust? Why do You keep believing that we will truly understand the importance of The One and begin our journey back Home some moment, some day, some lifetime? That we are not the body but the spirit within the body and when we begin to realize this, not intellectually but truly from within, then everything changes; all priorities are measured for their inherent worth under the vigilance of the spirit.

I know You are with us. I know that Your hands may be bound often due to the watertight workings of the law of cause and effect, the realm of karma. I know You must be hurt when we get a thrashing of our lives, either due to the past catching up with us, due to our own free will gone wrong or just our inherent self-destructive streak. I know there are times when You have to stand by the sidelines while we have our nose rubbed into the ground and life kicked out of us. Often, the very heavens have to stand by and watch the cleansing.

I know Baba Sai, that You truly love each one of us. Whether we deserve Your love or not does not matter to You, as You believe we all are One, have come from The One and shall merge with The One. I guess the motto of You and all the Masters is simple. Do not leave anybody behind.

I know Your presence in our lives is not some illusion or play of some feel-good, self-suggestive therapy. You are real.

That is my only reality. If there is something I would wager my very soul on, it is about You being with us whenever we want You to be there. That You are real and with each one of us, irrespective of whether we deserve it or not. We just need You to be with us. You and Your army of workers-devotees-children-Angels are with us. The day You say that this one is mine, a bond for eternity and beyond is forged, which can't be separated by anything.

I know many must truly chant Your name, through day and night, whenever time permits or when life becomes like a monsoon sky, dark as night. You hear each one of us who truly calls out to You with heart and soul and love, and as a child calling out to one's parent. I know this is the truth.

I know it truly hurts You when somebody is slandering us, spreading lies, hate or gossip. You have often said how nothing hurts You more than when people gossip, slander or fight. But then we will always remain self-absorbed in our own self-destruction. You have said that those who indulge in backbiting, slander and gossip wash away our dark karmas and lighten our burden by default. They darken their auras and release us from going through angst, hurt and pain of a more real kind. But only if we conduct ourselves with dignity will this make any sense. If we react and get down to the level of those who indulge in tarnishing and slandering, then we only complicate the karmic blueprint. Thus, even when somebody does any wrong to us, You have assured us that if we maintain a dignified silence, our detractors help us immensely by lightening our karmic load. You have compared these people who slander to pigs who eat their own shit. Thus, You want us to pray for those who help us tremendously, though by default.

So when somebody deceives, hurts or violates us, the individual helps us lighten our karmic load. If we go through it with dignity, it makes You truly happy and proud. It does not matter if there is spiritual truth in this or if it is a way of telling us that what needs to be gone through should be experienced with calmness. The fact is that this journey becomes worthwhile knowing that You know all that we go through. It makes this journey bearable. Sufferable. Knowing that You are aware. If You still have not done anything, it means You have given us Your permission to go through the ordeal. Knowing that You are with us through the pain, the angst, the humiliation and the heartache gives us the strength to plod on with our head held high.

Be it the death of a loved one or failure, You are standing by our side going through our pain as we are Your children. As our father and mother and all relationships rolled into one, I refuse to believe that You do not feel our pain. Even if the pain comes forth from attachment to the senses or ignorance, our pain is as real to us as the spirit world is to You. You are aware of this and You carry us, if we allow You to, through our angst and heartbreak.

You have told us to go through whatever is in store for us gracefully. But Baba, You do not seem to realize that in reality, we are conducting ourselves with grace because we want to make You happy and proud of us. Who cares about grace or whatever. It is You who matter and what You think and feel is paramount. You know this I hope. Your kids don't care a rat's arse about grace. It is You and You and only You we care about.

You are aware that for Your devotees, even the heaven does not hold a candle to You. Who wants heaven? We want You. You are the One, who time and again, guides us to give importance to our duty rather than drowning in the myriad by-lanes of the senses. To do one's lot honestly and leave the rest to You. There are various paths for yogis like meditation and Kundalini. For us, Your name is the seven dimensions and the three worlds of Lord Brahma, Lord Vishnu and Lord Shiva. You are our Trinity. You are our Goddess. You are the mantra, the pronunciation, the vibrations and the pause between the words.

We love you Baba. Have mercy on us and never let go of us. We are messed up with varying degrees of stupidity and self-destructiveness. Bear with us. Someday we are going to make You smile and make You proud. Till then puff deeply from Your chillum to calm Your darling nerves. Do not give up on us. We are Yours. Do as You wish. Make us feel Your presence just once in a while. You know we are as spiritually sensitive as the nearest lamp post, alien to all this psychic, spiritual and paranormal stuff. So please give us obvious signs of Your presence. Come to us when we are asleep in our dreams, and hug us tight or if in a hurry, just pat our heads. Even a warm 'What's up bachha?' would be more than cool. And yes, do us a favour, let us remember the dream for God's sake.

Ok Baba Sai, I would like to believe that You have read this inane rambling. If You haven't, not good, not good. Please read it. Please never forget that however flawed we may be, we are Yours.

Jai Baba my Sai. Jai Baba my Baba.

I know Baba Sai that You truly love each one of us. Whether we deserve Your love or not does not matter to You, as You believe we all are One and we all have come from The One and shall merge with The One.

I guess the motto of You and all the Masters is simple. Do not leave anybody behind.

When somebody deceives, hurts or violates us, the individual helps us lighten our karmic load.

Knowing that You are with us through the pain, the angst, the humiliation and the heartache gives us the strength to plod on with our head held high.

For us, Your name is the seven dimensions and the three worlds of Lord Brahma, Lord Vishnu and Lord Shiva. You are our Trinity. You are our Goddess. You are the mantra, the pronunciation, the vibrations and the pause between the words.

28

Do Yourself a Favour and Forgive

For me, spirituality, divinity and goodness are based on the foundations of selfless love, compassion and forgiveness. Yes, faith, patience, wisdom, prayers and meditation are most important, but they are a part of the selfless love already mentioned.

Compassion and forgiveness walk hand in hand. You cannot be a compassionate human being and not be forgiving by nature. It is like practicing the art of non-violence with hate and anger brewing within.

If one claims to have compassion or empathy and consideration, and still holds on to a grudge or the desire for violent justice or hate, then there is something amiss in one's understanding of compassion.

First of all, what is the meaning of forgiveness? According to me, it is the understanding that it is the circumstances that make an individual behave in a manner that causes hurt, grief or exhibits signs of ingratitude. And that the individual comes from the right place, but those circumstances got the better of the individual, forcing the person to behave in a manner not befitting his/her true self.

When you give the other person the benefit of doubt or another chance, or try to understand the individual's circumstances, state of desperation or mind frame, you have a more humane approach to the person and what caused him/her grief or angst.

That means you have in a way put yourself in the other person's shoes and embraced the philosophy that we all are human and being human, it is not uncommon for one to slip, mess up or behave in a manner that could cause hurt to somebody else.

I have hurt many people and thus in a strange way, I have learnt to be more open to others' flaws. So by default, falling has made me compassionate of those on the spiritual mat.

Also, if one believes in God, then belief in the laws of cause and effect and karma becomes mandatory; if one believes in God, one has to then unconditionally believe that our God is a just God, and if you believe in a just God, then there is no escaping the laws of karma.

So if somebody has hurt or deceived me, I would like to believe that somewhere, in some lifetime, I have initiated this relationship of hurt and deceit and thus I am being paid in the same coin to balance my karmic account. Or maybe it is a test to see how far I have walked on the spiritual path or to see if I can put into practice all that I preach. And boy, do I preach.

Also when we forgive, we are doing ourselves the greatest favour as then we let go of hatred, anger, violent thoughts, sadness, irritation and all these negative emotions which are like a virus, a form of cancer, that not only eat away our peace of mind but also our health, personality, joy and darken our soul and aura. Not to forgive means to live a life carrying a cross which will eventually break our spiritual backs and also take us away from selfless love and compassion, the two pillars that are so dear to the Lord.

When we hold a grudge against an individual, we are building further karma with him/her. When you give a poor person, even a beggar, a little money, and if you seek something in return, maybe appreciation, gratitude or even blessings, you begin a chain of karma with the individual, even if it is generated only through thought and not necessarily expressed. This will necessitate one to come down again in the body to balance off the debt. So says the law of karma.

It is only when you give selflessly that the laws of karma does not apply. The good deed will be passed on without the individuals getting involved. The laws of karma have been so fine-tuned by God with ample time at His/Her disposal.

Now imagine if one is seeking justice or revenge or not being able to forgive. Logic demands that the individual will have to return by putting a halt to his/her spiritual journey, just to seek a balancing of accounts. What a sad reason to encage one's being in the mire of illusions.

Let us do ourselves a humongous favour and release ourselves from the cesspool of cause and effect, and also from the claws of hate, revenge, harshness and sadness.

To forgive does not obviously mean to allow people to take advantage of you. Be aware and cautious. In no ancient text has it been advocated that one has to leave our senses and common sense to be spiritual.

If we cannot forgive, then what right do we have to seek forgiveness from the Big Boy up there? Logic demands that if you believe in eye for an eye, then be ready to lose an eye, or both, or worse, your spiritual vision.

Forgive. It is the most humane as well as the most sensible act to practice. Do not let the wrath of our Lord descend, as the

Big Boy will serve you a dish which you would want to be dished out to somebody else.

Be blessed always.

> *Compassion and forgiveness walk hand in hand. You cannot be a compassionate human being and not be forgiving by nature. It is like practicing the art of non-violence with hate and anger brewing within.*
>
> *When we forgive, we are doing ourselves the greatest favour as then we let go of hatred, anger, violent thoughts, sadness, irritation and all these negative emotions which are like a virus, a form of cancer, that not only eat away our peace of mind but also our health, personality, joy and darken our soul and aura.*
>
> *It is only when you give selflessly that the laws of karma does not apply. The good deed will be passed on without the individuals getting involved.*

29

Lord Ganesha . . . the Pathway
to the Goddess

According to me, the entire story of Lord Ganesha's birth and the chopping off of His Head is symbolic. If it did take place, then there is a reason which is far more spiritual than what it is made out to be.

The story of Lord Ganesha, as we have been told, goes something like this. Maa Parvati decides to have somebody of Her own, whose very existence will be to love and be there for Her, and obey Her word. So she applies a paste on Her body, removes the paste and creates Lord Ganesha. One day, wanting to have a bath in peace, She tells Her Son, Ganesha, that He should not let anybody enter the house.

He does just that. Nobody is allowed to enter. Even in the likeliness of a war, nobody is allowed to enter. He defeats all. When Lord Shiva tries to enter, He too is politely told to take a walk. Lord Shiva tries to reason with Ganesha, but when He realizes that there is no way this Child is going to even allow Him to enter, He chops off the Boy's head with His Trishul.

Maa Parvati comes out and witnesses Her Son lying on the floor with His Head chopped off. She decides to take the form of Maa Kali and destroy all of Creation. All the Gods reason with Maa and assure Her that Her Son will come back to life. An elephant, strolling along, finds its head relieved off its body and it is fixed to the Child's body. That is how we have Lord Ganesha as we know Him.

As a child I could never understand this story. I mean, we are talking about Lord Shiva. The knower of all. Are we seriously daring to suggest that He was unaware of such an important part of His and Maa's life? Even if He was in deep meditation, He is the knower of all, so there is no way He would be unaware of such an important event. Now let us assume that for some reason He was unaware of Lord Ganesha's birth. Even then, are we trying to assume that He had such little control over His anger and ego that He chopped off a Child's head? I mean, if Gods go about chopping heads when denied admission, how does one expect vermin mankind to practice restraint? As a child I could never fathom why He had to chop off an innocent baby elephant's head. How could the head of a large elephant fit a small child? Why chop off the head when all the three Gods—Lord Shiva, Lord Vishnu and Lord Brahma—were present? All They had to do was restore Lord Ganesha's original head using Their powers. But no, They had to resort to another act of violence. If the first act of violence was due to anger and ego, cutting off the elephant's head was an unmitigated disaster. Just as saying a lie a hundred times does not make it the truth, bringing forth life by killing something does not speak of either spirituality or Godhood.

So this story did not make sense to me. There had to be something deeper, something saner, something more real to this story.

This is what I believe. If you are reading this rambling of mine, it means two things. First, you are aware of the Chakras and the Kundalini. Second, you have a lot of spare time or nothing better to do.

What are Chakras? They are supposedly the energy centres situated on our ethereal bodies that correspond to various organs in our physical body. So the Heart Chakra also corresponds to the region of the physical heart in the body.

We have seven Chakras. Six are associated with the body while the seventh, the Crown Chakra, floats a few inches above our fat heads, not associated with our body but with the Eternal Truth, the pathway to self-realization.

The energy resides in the Root Chakra, which is dormant. The main purpose of life, as we know it, is to make this energy or Shakti or Kundalini rise, go through each Chakra and then reside in the Crown Chakra. Many wise folks claim that there are many Chakras, but as I can barely even make sense of Google Maps, there is no way I can make out the path to all the Chakras. Just suffice it to say that we have seven Chakras, various satellite Chakras and then more beyond the seventh Chakra, but as I still have trouble understanding where my gall bladder is, let us just get to the main point.

The Root Chakra is called the Muladhar Chakra. Each Chakra has a symbol, colour, sound and other stuff. I say not from experience but from what the Perfect Masters have told us. So the symbol of the Muladhar Chakra or the Root Chakra is an elephant, which in Hinduism is the form of Lord Ganesha. Thus, He is considered to be the God or the Gatekeeper of this Chakra. The Gatekeeper one must cross to reach the Goddess. The seat of all Kundalini Power or Shakti reposes in the Muladhar Chakra. The gate to this Chakra needs to be opened for the Kundalini, the Cosmic Energy, the Goddess Energy, the energy of no beginning and no end, the source and destination of all knowledge and Oneness, to begin its journey to the Crown Chakra and beyond, to self-realization, to *Aum Tat Sat* (I Am That), to the realm of Oneness.

So for the Kundalini to rise, the Muladhar Chakra has to be activated. This Chakra is also associated with earthiness, our survival instinct and the need for the external. The Goddess Energy lies dormant as the mind is preoccupied with the gross and not the subtle, and certainly not Oneness and the union of Shiv Shakti.

Till this Chakra is not shaken up, the Shakti will remain dormant. The petty ego, the gross, the temporary and the mundane resides in the mind, the mind in the consciousness, the consciousness in the brain and the brain in one's fat head. Till this ego is chopped off—till the head filled with the gross is not annexed—there is no way the individual can make his/her way up towards self-realization and Oneness.

So Shiva, the Yogi, the Big Boy, has no option but to chop off the false ego that is associated with the gross. Thus Shiva chops of the Boy's head. The Goddess goes into a rage. This means the Shakti which has been lying dormant begins to move. This Shakti is a billion times more powerful than all the nuclear bombs put together. If this energy is not channelled in the right direction, it can create havoc. Maa Parvati takes on the form of Maa Kali, the one who destroys. The only way to prevent destruction is to find another head for the Boy. The false ego has been chopped off, but there is the need for another head to be able to first and foremost hold the Pure Ego or the Pure Consciousness. Then that Pure Consciousness needs a channel, tunnel, pipe or trunk to take that energy and direct it upward, through the other Chakras, to reside with the Mother. The Elephant's head is thus a symbolic representation of a vehicle that can sustain and contain the energy, and the trunk is the tunnel through which this energy can be channelled upward.

As no spiritual growth can take place without chopping off the head of false ego and directing the consciousness up towards Mother Energy, the most auspicious of all things in Creation, we pray to Lord Ganesha before embarking on a new venture. All good can take place only through Him. Energy needs to be pure and that pure energy needs to be channelled upwards; energy in its original form is neither pure nor impure.

When energy is used for sexual release, we term that energy sexual energy, but if it is used to work towards spiritualism, that very energy, which could have been discharged, leads to self-realization. The energy is the same, the way we use it defines its destination, potential and capabilities.

Even Lord Brahma and Lord Vishnu could not calm Goddess Parvati from destroying the world by taking the form of Maa Kali. This is for the simple reason that Lord Vishnu is the Preserver. As a Preserver, He could never fathom that sometimes death or destruction is instrumental for true change. As an individual, our sole purpose is survival and often spiritual growth or perseverance goes against worldly growth and survival. Thus, Lord Vishnu could be of no help here.

Lord Brahma is the Creator. We are talking about the destruction or death of the false ego here. We want to create a life that is filled with what appeases our senses. Going within and taking the energy upward goes against the reasoning for creating wealth, power and success. Thus He too could never fathom death of one's self or the false ego for moving upwards.

It is Lord Shiva, the Eternal Yogi, the Transformer or crudely put, the Destroyer, who knew that for true growth, something had to be annexed, something had to die or be chopped away. He went ahead and did it, even though it was His own Son. We have both Lord Shiva and Maa Parvati residing within us as yin and yang. It is when we take on the role of Lord Shiva, the Transformer, that we can take decisions. Thus it is the individual who has to first destroy the false ego for the real ego, the True Consciousness, to emerge. And that is why Lord Shiva cuts off Ganesha's head. That is why we need to cut off the false head which is steeped in the gross and endow oneself with the True Consciousness.

Lord Ganesha is the possessor of True Consciousness. The Boy's head had to be cut off. So did the elephant's head, as it was meant for a higher purpose. One does not just need a large container but also True Consciousness and the knowledge to take this energy up. The Boy had the knowledge and the love for the Mother, the true seat of Creation and Consciousness, but needed a better container and the elephant provided that.

So, one has to cut off the false ego, go within, and take the energy upward. That is why the Muladhar Chakra is called the Root Chakra; if the root is not strong, nothing is going to hold for long. The elephant has four feet, which means you need a solid foundation, and a trunk that can go skyward towards Mommy.

This is my understanding of Lord Ganesha. I could be completely off the radar but then each one has his/her perception of reality and Oneness.

Be blessed always.

The symbol of the Muladhar Chakra or the Root Chakra is an elephant, which in Hinduism is the form of Lord Ganesha. Thus, He is considered to be the God or the Gatekeeper of this Chakra. The Gatekeeper one must cross to reach the Goddess.

Pure Consciousness needs a channel, tunnel, pipe or trunk to take that energy of Pure Consciousness and direct it upward, through the other Chakras, to reside with the Mother. The Elephant's head is thus a symbolic representation of a vehicle that can sustain and contain the energy, and the trunk is the tunnel through which this energy can be channelled upward.

As no spiritual growth can take place without chopping off the head of false ego and directing the consciousness up towards Mother Energy, the most auspicious of all things in Creation, we pray to Lord Ganesha before embarking on a new venture. All good can take place only through Him.

One has to cut off the false ego, go within, and take the energy upward. That is why the Muladhar Chakra is called the Root Chakra; if the root is not strong, nothing is going to hold for long. The elephant has four feet, which means you need a solid foundation, and a trunk that can go skyward towards Mommy.

30

Spiritual Totality

Channelling has given me the opportunity to interact with innumerable people, week after week, for over sixteen years now. I started out when I was twenty eight or twenty-nine and now I am nearing fifty. None the wiser, but enriched after having learnt about individuals who have opened their hearts and lives to me.

Yes, after the work has been done, there are many who have never kept in touch, but that is understandable. Why would you keep in touch with a doctor once you have been cured or the illness has worsened? No matter for what reason people have walked into my channelling room, the fact is that they have enriched my life more than I have theirs.

I only wish I could answer more letters, phone messages and be there more for those in need, but I know am failing miserably in this department. I am trying my best and I know that my best is not enough. It isn't for the want of effort or inclination. My silence has infuriated some reasonably sane folks to behave in an unreasonable manner, but I guess for each one of us, our problems require immediate attention and if that does not happen, our anger gets projected in the form unbecoming conduct.

So if I have in any way made anybody feel neglected or ignored, I am sorry.

As usual, I have rambled on from what I wanted to convey. So here goes. I have realized that spirituality means different things to different people.

There is a large, growing populace who are into the field of Light and energy, meditation, Kundalini, Chakras, crystals and various methods of healing. They are experiencing various visions and communications, even miracles, and I am truly happy for each one of them. For them, spirituality is the realm of the ethereal. They believe in two worlds, one of the physical and then of life after death, auras and one-to-one communication with the Lord, Goddess, Master, Angels, and various resident and non-resident spirits of the netherworld. The inherent issue with this part of the world is that very often real visions co-exist with the play of the subconscious and the power of suggestions; the by-lanes where reality ends and illusions begin are very strong and real, making many of this sweet breed as cuckoo as a clock.

Then there is a section which believes that all this talk about the paranormal is poppycock and they do not think much of all this esoteric stuff. They look aghast when they hear about anybody who believes or indulges in 'esoteric mumbo jumbo'. Their philosophy of spirituality involves hard-core charity and spreading the Light by offering financial help. They are convinced that feeding a hungry mouth is far better than all the intellectual or paranormal stuff floating about, very often making this section encaged in their own intellectual or do-gooder power play.

I have a huge group that only walks the path of destiny and ascribes to the laws of karma. They believe that neither healing, energy, work or charity is going to make any difference, as what is destined is destined and each one has his/her karmic blueprint to experience, crosses to carry, mountains to climb, family jewels to be nailed to the ground and tears to shed. One can only go about it calmly and wisely, and try to get done with this backlog and not create new nonsense. Spirituality is going through karma like a woman goes through the pangs of child birth . . . the pain is mind-numbing and excruciating but yet joyous . . . as all is going to be worth it with the birth of the child. For one and all, the baby may look suspiciously similar to a disgruntled squirrel, yet for the mommy, he/she is more beautiful than all the Angels put together. The fear of becoming fatalistic or even cold to the problems of others is a reality, where individual free will ceases to exist. I have seen sensible folks succumb to the power of the philosophy, 'what has to happen will happen, so why stretch beyond a point'. This makes them annoyingly fatalistic to the point of becoming cold to the hurt and pain of others.

Then there are those who believe in prayers and chanting. For them, spirituality is equivalent to the time spent in prayer. The more they pray, the more they feel closer to Goddess, God and Guru. They may or may not believe in all the varied spiritual paths, but for them, prayer and more prayer is the way to embrace The One. You can either personally or via skype communicate with your Master and do all the charity, but they believe it is prayers and chanting that is going to lead to one's salvation. I believe in this path too but one has to give one's best and pray for the right reasons, being aware that very often prayers might soften the blow, but the blow is not going away any time soon. Getting disillusioned with The One for not answering prayers is something I have seen happen more often than not. It is heartbreaking to see somebody throw in the towel and become an agnostic or even an atheist just because their prayers have not been answered the way they want them to be.

Then we have those who do not believe in charity but are convinced that giving themselves to serve those in need and the less privileged is the way forward towards their Lord. They believe in physically pushing the borders of their will and endurance, and breaking their backs to bring back the smiles and laughter in those who had forgotten joy and comfort. Very often, they look down upon those who pray, follow rituals or practice esoteric healing or communication with the other side.

And then there is a certain section which believes in all the ways mentioned above and strives to reach The One using every pathway, unprejudiced to any of the above highways of spirituality. He/she is certain that to be the perfect disciple, one has to assimilate each of the above mentioned ways of spirituality and stitch them all into one humble cloak, and walk the path. He/she doesn't care to judge or debate the superiority of one path, but uses every by-lane, every nook, every crevice, every ravine and peak—whatever it takes to put a smile on his/her God, Goddess and Guru. I like this group. Any and every way to please The One is indulged in, as long as they have given their best to please the Boss Man up there.

For me, spirituality is like the sun. Agastya Rishi, who gave Lord Ram the famous hymn in praise of the sun, the *Aditya Hridaya Stotra*, just before the Lord went to battle Ravana and his army, was clear that the sun was the embodiment of all that which was good, noble and divine. There are seven different types of rays or colours that come forth from the sun, each embodied with a characteristic; it takes all seven rays or colours in unison to bring forth the divinity of the sun.

Similarly, I believe all the paths of spirituality are unique in their singularity and individuality. One needs to embrace every aspect and every path, not looking down upon any, certain that there is a unifying thread which passes through every path, all leading eventually through that one door.

Even the yogi who meditates in the Himalayas is serving all of mankind as the vibrations emitted through his meditation first sends forth ripples and then waves upon waves of well-being, peace, tranquillity and harmony for all of Creation. If the yogi was only concerned about his/her own salvation and thought that the rest of Creation could go boil their ludicrous heads, his/her journey for salvation would be slow and arduous, taking lifetimes. It will have its fair share of trials, cramps, arthritis and haemorrhoids. But the moment the yogi seeks not just his/her salvation, but the peace and well-being of all of Creation, the cosmos smiles and helps the spiritual mule to achieve not only his/her own goal but also help all of Creation.

All the Masters first put the well-being of all of Creation before Their personal interest. The very fact that Masters do not take the final leap into the Great Fire that allows Them to merge with The One and thus become The One is because They love Their children so much. They want to help them to merge, and only then would Their work be complete. The great Master Tajuddin Baba was very clear when He said that till He did not help in creating 1,20,000 saints on earth, He would not rest or take the final step towards the liberation of one's own self by merging with The One——call it Mukti, Moksha, merging or whatever.

Thus, all spirituality has to be holistic and not individualistic. If we meditate or pray only for oneself or one's near and dear ones and not for one and all, it means we adhere to the philosophy of diversity and individuality and not true Oneness. If our prayers do not involve those not in our orbit—the unfortunate, the dying, the starving, the meek, the damned, the bullied, the tortured, the ailing, the lonely, the homeless, the heartbroken, the earth bound, the defeated, the left behind, those in the physical plane, those in the spirit plane and those in between—we are driving a stationary car. Not moving in reality. If each moment is not spent in spreading the Light and compassion of The One, then there is something we are doing wrong. Just prayers. Just charity. Just visions. Remains just that . . . just. It has to be a composition, a symphony of all the right notes using all the right sounds by all the right instruments played by you, the musician. If we do not use every bit of our self with a little of all that we have got, then the scenery keeps changing due to the illusionary projector behind while we remain rooted to the same spot. This is like those olden-day photography studios where one sat in cutouts of cars and planes and got photographed with changing backdrops of monuments, snow mountains, beach and the like. In reality, it was just like shadow-boxing. Nobody went anywhere.

Whether you communicate with your God, Goddess and Guru or every known and unknown spirit in Creation; whether you pray or heal or provide financial help or your own time, the essence of spirituality is enriching each moment, not just yours and mine but all those with whom we associate directly or indirectly. It needs to be embraced in its totality. It is like the ingredients in a meal that is required in a minuscule quantum——so minuscule that a bystander might think it really makes no difference, but the chef knows that every ingredient helps in creating a master dish. Similarly, spirituality is all about embracing and unifying. The sun would lose its radiance if one of the seven rays were missing from it.

I understand that all of us cannot do everything. There are some who truly can't contribute financially as they themselves are trying their best to keep their body and spirit together. But they can give off their goodness, their kindness and their smile by just being decent individuals, spreading love, laughter and tenderness. Their contribution or charity or projection of compassion may not be in cash or kind or even their time, but of their very essence and that divine spark that lurks in each one of us. A short prayer for the well-being of those going through pain and discomfort of various intensities does not take too much of time. Chanting in the mind while going about one's day takes only love and discipline. Keeping silent within is our natural state and the most profound method of meditation.

In early days and even today, we can see this kind of spirituality where a woman or a man takes care of a home in a manner that is so simple but still so pure, making life and home a place of worship. I am sure that most of us have had somebody in our lives or family who were, without even knowing it, more spiritual than most, including the so-called present Masters.

Spirituality in all its totality is the only way to go forward on this beautifully infuriating journey back home. For me, the very word 'spirituality' comes forth from living a life knowing that one comes forth from the Great Spirit, which makes one 'spiritual' and to give each moment one's true essence in all its 'totality'. Spiritual in totality——when you marry these two words, you get spirituality.

Be blessed always.

There are seven different types of rays or colours that come forth from the sun, each embodied with a characteristic. But it takes all seven rays or colours in unison to bring forth the divinity of the sun.

All the paths of spirituality are unique in their singularity and individuality. One needs to embrace every aspect and every path, not looking down upon any, certain that there is a unifying thread which passes through every path, all leading eventually through that one door.

All spirituality has to be holistic and not individualistic. If we meditate or pray only for oneself or one's near and dear ones and not for one and all, it means we adhere to the philosophy of diversity and individuality and not true Oneness.

If each moment is not spent in spreading the Light and compassion of The One, then there is something we are doing wrong. Just prayers. Just charity. Just visions. Remains just that . . . just.

The very word 'spirituality' comes forth from living a life knowing that one comes forth from the Great Spirit, which makes one 'spiritual' and to give each moment one's true essence in all its 'totality'. Spiritual in totality—when you marry these two words, you get spirituality.

31

Dignity of It All . . .

Every now and then I get to hear well-crafted yarns or deranged narratives about myself. People seem to have a lot of time in hand or extreme emptiness in the heart. Some very imaginative stuff has been spoken and spread, and I have realized that some folks are truly gifted with the art of storytelling and are wasting their talent by not getting into mainstream fiction.

I am certain that you must have found yourself at the other end of the stick too, and very often wondered how and why people have so much of time in hand. You also wonder at the emptiness of their heart and soul that makes them conjure and spread such compost.

But then if you and I look a little inward, we realize that we are not free from this sickness of mudslinging, slander and backstabbing either. If we try to recollect just the past seven days of all that we have said and done, I am sure we will find words which we have spoken or thought of which we are not proud of. We realize that we too indulge in slander, gossip and spreading filth, maybe in a lesser degree. We are all grouchy peas in the

203

same pod. I doubt if any of us can claim otherwise. We are all in various degrees involved in spreading some vicarious filth, true or completely false or largely modified, about some poor innocent bastard.

The power to slander, gossip and malign is so inherent in each one of us in various degrees that we have made billionaires out of a few people, set up economies and helped make the world as small as a village, through platforms like Facebook and Twitter.

Have you truly wondered why social media is so immensely popular? The need to shoot our mouths off about ourselves or pass random comments safely cushioned behind a name which may be true or not, without being seen, seems to be a part of human nature. Throwing a stone from the comfort and invisibility of a mob has been a practice since Stone Age. And how ridiculously easy it is to slander using these various social media. Of course, not everyone uses these platforms for verbal diarrhoea, but you know what I mean.

What I have realized is that sometimes in our habit or foolishness we may say certain things that may come to haunt us. It may become a very heavy cross to carry as rumours, slander and malicious gossip have its own life, its own claws and its own wayward destiny. A friend of mine committed suicide as somebody began to spread rumours about his sexual preference. The poor boy was effeminate in appearance, but his sexual needs had no gay tinge to it. His mother heard the rumour, believed it and swallowed some sleeping pills. She was rushed to the intensive room in Breach Candy Hospital in a critical condition and our friend jumped off the fourth floor in shock, guilt and anger. The mother survived. He didn't.

I remember spending weeks in a state of guilt and hell, trying to remember if even unintentionally I had ever fanned the already floating rumours. I knew I had not once cared or spoken about all this as a person's sexual preference is his/her own, and if the same gender lights one's bulb, more power to you.

Baba Sai of Shirdi has compared those who spread lies, gossip or rumours to pigs who like to eat their own excrement. No matter how well you feed a swine or pig, eventually they will feast on their own shit for dessert.

Then there is the other issue which has spread like plague amongst us . . . the poor-me syndrome. Playing the victim. No matter what happens, blame one and all. The firm belief that one can speak or do no wrong and that being naturally flawless, the blame lies with the other individual or the world at large. In the worst case scenario, when one can't possibly blame anybody, then the fault has to lie with the planets.

I have seen so many families go through misery because there is one person in that family whose very purpose and reason of existence is to make life a living hell for the others, irrespective of caste, sex or creed. No matter what you do, the sacrifices, the large-heartedness, the indulgences or the overlooking, one thing is certain: that particular individual is going to find faults, criticize, mock and take the fizz out as he/she refuses to see the Light. For that, he/she would need to take his/her fat head out of one of the anatomical extremities.

So the question is why do we do the things that we do, like slander and playing the victim, knowing very well that we are spreading sadness, negativity, anger, hate and tears like a stench? God alone knows what this does to our karmic blueprint. Yes, God, Goddess and Guru will always be with us, but what a sad place to make Them reside. In a shell which breeds slander or/and is perpetually playing the victim. I read this profound statement the other day. It goes something like this . . . 'Jesus loves you, but it is everybody else who thinks you are an asshole.'

So it got me wondering why we do what we do, even though in every other department we may come out smelling of roses. I have known such people. They truly are great or even noble in every other department. But like a person who slogs and prepares a meal for a hundred people with all sincerity and love and then goes and spits in the dish, they have one of these two issues or God forbid, both these two cardinal, though underrated and overlooked evils.

Well, the reasons for such behaviour are for another day. As of now, I truly want to understand if I belong to either of the two categories.

These two habits are so underrated and overlooked that we often consider them as normal behaviour, but the fact of it all is that God is in the details and the devil is in the small print.

Be blessed always.

> *God is in the details and the devil is in the small print.*
>
> *In our habit or foolishness, we may sometimes say certain things that may come to haunt us or become a very heavy cross to carry.*

32

Avatar Meher Baba and His Final Warning—Strength of Silence

Avatar Meher Baba ki jai. We chant this mantra in remembrance and praise of Meher Baba. He left His body on 31 January. Or did He? Perfect Masters and Avatars never leave. They always have been and will remain.

Meher Baba was silent for forty-three years and kept insisting throughout His life that He would break His silence. He never did. Even during the two body-breaking accidents, He never uttered a word. Ostensibly, He did not keep His word.

Why would He insist that He would speak and then deny all of Creation the sound of His beautiful voice? Did He change His mind? Did He see the futility of speaking to a world that is deaf or insists on not listening? Or did Meher Baba break His silence before He left His body?

What does it mean 'to speak' or 'break one's silence'? Does it mean to vocally express oneself or to make people listen and stop being deaf to the glory, mercy and grace of one's God, Goddess and Guru? If it is the latter, then yes, Meher Baba has kept His word, as through these decades there have been more and more people who have loved Him, heard Him, seen Him, obeyed Him and followed Him. He has graced them through dreams, miracles, oracles, psychics, mediums, and through ways and means the Perfect Ones communicate with Their children.

This whole business of silence needs to be understood with more intent and clarity. Silence is the sound of the Creator. He/She manifests through silence. There is no greater or more potent force in all of Creation as silence. The fact that Meher Baba communicated through sign language and His writings and books meant that He was communicating; He wasn't exactly silent. But for mankind, only when an individual refuses to talk vocally does it mean that he/she is on the path of silence. Thus, I do not believe that Meher Baba was silent. He spoke, but we were, are and will continue to be deaf.

Do we follow Meher Baba? If yes, then we should be as silent as the tomb within. We should refrain from slander. We should turn our backs on all acrimony and gibberish, within and outside. But no, we don't do any of these things. But yes, we will talk softly when we are near Baba's Samadhi, or worse, some 'holy-than-thou' caretaker of the Samadhi will make sure nobody talks, or children don't play or giggle . . . why? . . . because Meher Baba kept silent . . . or He did not like joy and laughter . . . or expression of love for Him, Mehera Maa and the mandali through words. During *aarti*, anybody can sing and play musical instruments . . . no matter how out of tune . . . but otherwise, 'thou shall not speak'.

Our assumptions on silence are so off the radar that I can very well imagine Meher Baba using the choicest Zoroastrian swear words to express His disgust.

In 1968, Meher Baba issued a few points in the form of 'The Last Warning'. The first of these was that we should hold on to Baba's *daman* (piece of clothing) till the very end.

What does that mean? Keep the faith. Don't let doubt make you wander hither and thither like a headless chicken. When things get rough or we make things rough by engaging in mental calculations, or our faith is based on give and take with one's Master, we tend to move away from The One and the path. Meher Baba hence made it clear that one must not move away from the Master and His/Her path.

Then, there was a warning 'to not get intimately involved with one's family affairs and to not be emotionally upset by such things'. What does this mean? Does it mean one should be detached from one's family? Or does it mean when one is too entangled with one's family, one ceases to think calmly and become centred? When one is not centred and calm, one can fall off the path and make blunders and create karmas, which could take eons to burn away.

The next warning was 'to forgive and forget one another's trespasses'. This seems quite clear, but unfortunately we seem only to forgive and forget our own trespasses and certainly not of anybody else. Forgiveness and forgetting comes forth from compassion and humility. Good luck with that.

Then, 'one should not succumb to lust'. The word 'lust' is a strange animal. We usually attribute it to sexual gratification and the constant urge to indulge and experience physical intimacy. I am sure sex is a part of lust. But what is the exact meaning of lust? Is the all-consuming need and want of sex the only attribute of lust? What about the overpowering and all-consuming need, want and itch for power, money, importance and attention? I think lust means anything that is irrational and all-consuming, which could make an individual resort to the basest acts through the most obscene means.

Meher Baba then warns His lot 'to be less aggressive towards others and less tolerant towards themselves'. This is so beautifully put. We seem to be more aggressive towards one and all and perfectly comfortable in our skins even though in reality we should be skinned alive.

Being less aggressive towards others means one should come forth with compassion, love, largeness of heart and minimal or no judgement. Being less tolerant towards oneself means to not cloak all our bullshit in the garb of personal reasons, childhood trauma and poor-me syndrome.

We all are Baba lovers. But how many of us would have survived living with Baba? The mandali did because they allowed Meher Baba to push their ego into the warm embrace of Mother Earth. Meher Baba was a Spiritual Giant, and Giants are tyrants and dictators. They know what is best for Their lot. The only way to truly love The One is through complete obedience and surrender. If you cannot completely surrender your ego to The One, your love is self-centred. If you cannot implicitly obey The One with love and happiness, then your so-called obedience is nothing but a ruse, a show, manipulation.

Then comes—'to beware at all times of persons who lead others into believing that they are saintly and pious, and profess to possess supernatural powers. However pious such persons appear to be, a lover of Baba must never mix such piety with the divinity of the Avatar.' The lovers of Baba seem to have got this statement a bit mixed up. Baba has clearly said two things. People can wear a garb of spirituality, so be aware. Never mix any kind of piety and spirituality with the divinity of the Avatar. I do not think what Meher Baba meant was that all those who are walking the path are hypocrites. He made it clear that however spiritual an individual is, he/she can never match the divinity of the Avatar.

This is why mediums and psychics, however noble and pure, are just mediums and psychics. None of us can profess anything else other than being instruments of The One. I truly believe that most mediums and psychics are human beings, flawed and working on their respective karmas. Nothing more or nothing less.

Then Meher Baba says, 'a true Baba-lover must remember the repeated warning to stay away from persons who feel and assert that they are masters and saints, and possess powers to help human beings. His lovers and workers should never get involved with such persons, much less with perverted "helpers of humanity" who have no reverence or regard for the Perfect Masters and the Avatar of the age. Beware of those who exploit spirituality to gain their selfish ends and dupe others.'

This is again self-explanatory, but the latter half makes it ambiguous. Does this mean that a medium or a spiritual worker, who is not perverted or who has all the reverence and regard for the Perfect Masters and the Avatar of the age and does not exploit for personal gains, is somebody one can trust and go for guidance and help? How on earth does one know who is who in this time and age? Does that mean one should never seek help and guidance from such folks who may just truly be selfless and want to help mankind in the best way possible?

Does it mean all those who connect with the other world, through Masters or even loved ones who have passed over, are damned, as all those who indulge in any paranormal or occult activities have been damned by Meher Baba? He has clearly mentioned that only those who use this power for selfish purposes or to create a false aura around themselves should be avoided, but what about those who are truly trying to spread the Light?

Meher Baba lives in each one of His lovers. It is our duty to respect Him by walking the path. By being kind and helpful, and most importantly, by being compassionate and humane. All of us who wear the so-called spiritual garb seem to forget that the first pillar of spirituality is calm silence. Till we don't respect this, we can chant 'Jai Babas', but nothing is going to matter to Avatar Meher Baba.

That is why Meher Baba loved Mehera Maa. She loved Him silently, completely, selflessly and most importantly, with silent surrender and obedience.

Be blessed.

Avatar Meher Baba ki jai.

> *Silence is the sound of the Creator. He/She manifests through silence. There is no greater or more potent force in all of Creation as silence.*
>
> *Keep the faith. Don't let doubt make you wander hither and thither like a headless chicken. When things get rough or we make things rough by doing mental calculations, or our faith is based on give and take with one's Master, we tend to move away from The One and the path.*
>
> *Meher Baba lives in each one of His lovers. It is our duty to respect Him by walking the path. By being kind and helpful, and most importantly, compassionate and humane.*

33

Wake the Boss Up

We are a strange species. We are aware that the Sun does not rise or set, but still go about believing that it does. The fact that darkness envelops the place we live is because the earth has shown its back to the sun. These are simple truths we can learn, but for eons most of us have refused to do so.

Every religious text, scripture, God, Goddess and Guru, like a stuck gramophone, repeats the need to go within. The importance of solitude, silence, silent reflection, contemplation and meditation. I wonder why. Did They run out of new ideas? The present spiritual environment has new ideas cropping up every few days. New methods of tickling the Kundalini out of Her slumber abide. New methods of healing and DNA rejuvenation are introduced every now and then.

Our Giants appeared to have suffered from an overdose of obsessive compulsive disorder as They kept telling us to practise silence and meditate. Not to forget the usual rigmarole of God, Goddess and Guru that the secrets and wisdom of the Creator lay within each individual.

They did not talk about DNA, Kundalini, Chakras, teleporting or manifestations; all They kept harping about was to go within.

Either They truly did not know what our present lot is aware of or They were certain that the only way to salvation was to go within.

Go within and do what? I wonder. But no, go within, the voice says. I truly reside within. I try to go within and in a few seconds I am snoring my guts out. So either my 'within' is an oasis of sleep to be caught up with or I am going about this whole process like a truly wise, headless chicken.

Ok, so let us try and amuse the Giants by understanding this whole 'going within' tamasha.

This is what I have understood. Keep in mind that my schoolteachers would pray that I copied in my exams so that I would be promoted to the higher class. So my intelligence quotient has always been under suspect, but if you are reading my stuff, then it doesn't say much about your intelligence either. So let us just ramble and go for the ride within.

This is what I have understood. Every religion insists on chanting the name. So a Shiva devotee is told to chant 'Aum Namaha Shivaya' using one mala of 108 beads or to repeat it thrice or nine times. Or 'Maa Kali Namo Namo'. Or 'Jai Baba'. Or 'Satnam Wahe Guru'. Or 'Bismillah-E-Rehman-E-Rahim'. Or 'Hail Mary'. Or 'Ashem Vohu'. Take your pick.

Now the question to ask is: is our respective God, Goddess and Guru hard of hearing or on some major ego trip, loving the sound of His/Her name?

I mean, why would I want my child to go on chanting, 'Dad Dad Dad Dad'? Why would I want my name to be repeated so many times? After I hear her calling out my name more than once, I tell Meher, 'Baby, your dad is hard of hearing, but is not as deaf as a lamp post.'

So why are we told to sit quietly, adjust our pose and chant the name? We are told to focus on our breath and yeah right, do something with it. We have to focus on it entering and leaving our body . . . within seconds I am snoring my smoke-congested chest away, with my mouth open. Even if I observe the breath coming into my body and leaving through the various openings, I mean, how does that light my bulb?

I am told that the kingdom of heaven that lies within will be realized.

That easy, *haan*? How can it be? There are workshops that run for days teaching complicated stuff using powerpoint presentations and huge printouts . . . charging the price of a kidney and liver . . . and showing one how to raise the Kundalini or heal or soar . . . and here I am told to sit down like an unemployed thug and pass my day observing my breath going in and out. I have to chant the name till God, Goddess and Guru is so exasperated that He/She has no option but to come down and say, 'What the—'.

But in channelling, Baba Sai keeps saying this to one and all: 'Go within, beta . . . no, not to the other room . . . but within yourself . . . focus on your breath . . . beta, why have you stopped breathing? . . . chant the name . . . yes, I know you can't focus on the breath and chant the name loudly . . . chant in the mind, beta . . .'

And then, I got it. I sort of got it. So this is it. This is my understanding of it.

I am sure some other loser has already thought of it but who cares . . . I too got the gist on my own, or so I would like to believe.

We are not the body. We are the energy that resides in the body. A spark from the Great Flame. A drop from the Wide Ocean. A tune from the Groovy Orchestra. A sound from the Great Word.

Within us resides all that which resides in the Paramatma, the Boss, the Prime Soul.

Now even if I go within, focus on my breath and begin to chant the name, till I am not certain that I am not the body, my attention will always be external. So I may be 'within', but my search is external. I have in my mind the picture of my God, Goddess and Guru—a snap that I am attached to or the statue of Baba Sai in Shirdi. So even though my eyes are shut, I am breathing and chanting His name. My true being is outside me, external, with Baba Sai's statue in Shirdi or the photograph in front of me.

So in reality I am not within because I believe that Baba Sai is in Shirdi. Or Meher Baba is in Meherabad.

Thus, though I would like to believe I am internalizing, in reality, I am not. I believe that my Master, God or Goddess is outside me, so I am sitting like an unemployed manic ape, focusing on my breath and chanting the name.

I am waiting for the energy to fill me up. I am hoping for some sign. I am imagining I am with my Master. I am surging with bliss as I have felt some light or colour entering my body. But we are not internal, only external here.

When do I begin getting internal? When I know He/She already exists within me and I begin my search within. When I chant 'Aum Namaha Shivaya', 'Aum Sai Nath' or 'Jai Maa Kali', I am not calling out to The One, from outside, to come to me. No. I am doing the opposite. I am trying to wake The One who slumbers within me or clean the gross shit I have covered Him/Her with. I am trying to reactivate The One who already resides within me, as if I am the spark from the Great Flame. The Fire is already within us: all we have to do is activate the Spark, reignite the Fire, fan the Flame and make it into a raging Fire within.

So every time I chant 'Aum Namaha Shivaya', I believe that He already resides within me, and my duty, dharma and sole purpose in life is to bring forth His presence. It is to activate this presence which is now dormant within, so that you or I realize The One within, operate from It and may in some lifetime become The One within.

Thus you have been told to chant the name all the time; believe that you and The One are one.

By believing this and then chanting the name, going within and breathing, The One who is dormant in our spiritual DNA gets woken up, and then begins to operate from within. The more you wake up the Boss, the more He/She operates from within. We need to believe He/She resides within and through the chant—slow, meditative, focused, internalized—the connect will take place. We have to slowly wake Him/Her up. Like a child, we need to go on tenderly waking up our God, Goddess and Guru. The more we pray this way, you and I will one day feel The One within, and that will be the first step towards self-realization and all the mystical treasures one seeks on this path.

A point comes when you begin your meditation visualizing your God, Goddess and Guru and then after a few seconds or repetitions of the name, you go within and chant the name as though you are praying to yourself, aware that your One is within you and all one needs to do is activate that connect within you. Basically, wake up the Boss.

Then you need no pilgrimages. No paraphernalia. No pujari. No flame. No fruits. No flowers. Nothing. You are the devotee. You are the one praying to The One within you. So you are praying and being prayed to. You are the one chanting and being chanted to. You are The One.

That doesn't mean you or I will be able to do it any time soon. I wish we do but it might take eons. But that is not the point. Realization is overrated. It is operating from the realization that He/She is not out there anywhere but within; this is the most important step.

I meet folks who communicate with various Gods, Goddesses and Gurus, and I truly am happy for them. Can I bet my very soul that Baba Sai comes forth through me? No, I can't. I hope He does. Till we are not realized, we can never know what is going on. It is realization that brings about certainty in the spiritual realm.

But I know one thing. Every time you chant the name, search for The One within you. Not outside you. The moment you do that, you are going within and operating from being the Energy and not the body. Activate that dormant memory of you and The One as one. Wake the Boss up. He/She has been snoring for far too long.

Be blessed.

Jai Baba.

We are not the body. We are the energy that resides in the body. A spark from the Great Flame. A drop from the Wide Ocean. A tune from the Groovy Orchestra. A voice from the Great Word.

Within us resides all that which resides in the Paramatma, the Boss, the Prime Soul.

Thus you have been told to chant the name all the time; believe that you and The One are one.

We need to believe He/She resides within and through the chant— slow, meditative, focused, internalized—the connect will take place. We have to slowly wake Him/Her up. Like a child, we need to go on tenderly waking up our God, Goddess and Guru.